SHODEN

Marion McGeough
British Academy of Reiki

© Marion McGeough all rights reserved

All rights reserved. This book may not be reproduced, transmitted, or stored in whole or in part by any means including graphic, electronic or mechanical without expressed written consent of the publisher/author except in the case of brief quotations embodied in critical articles and reviews. The right of Marion McGeough to be identified as the author/owner of this work has been asserted by them in accordance with the Copyright, Designs and Patents Act 1988.

Published by Marion McGeough.

All rights reserved. No part of this publication may be reproduced, stored in a retrieval system or transmitted in any form or by any means, electronic, mechanical, photocopying, recording or otherwise without the prior permission of the publisher.

While the publisher has taken reasonable care in the preparation of this book, the publisher makes no representation, express or implied, with regard to the accuracy of the information contained in this book and cannot accept legal responsibility or liability for any errors or omissions from the book or the consequences thereof.

Products or services that are referred to in this book may be either trademarks and/or registered trademarks of their respective owners. The publisher and author make no claims to these trademarks.

A CIP Catalogue record for this book is available from the British Library.

Formatting and cover design by ebook-designs.co.uk

This is a work of fiction. The events and characters described herein are imaginary and are not intended to refer to specific places or living persons. The opinions expressed in this manuscript are solely the

opinions of the author.

DEDICATION

This book is dedicated to my Reiki students and clients who have helped me learn so much. You have all made me a much better, more humble person.

Thank You.

Marion McGeough

February 2014

REIKI: MY PERSONAL JOURNEY

I first discovered Reiki in 2009. I had experienced a number major life changing events including the death of my mother and other family members, personal health problems: mine as well as my husbands, and financial difficulties. My world felt as if it was falling apart. These events had all occurred in a period of less than 2 years. I had managed to grieve and it was now time to re-focus my attention by learning something new. As I searched the web I kept coming across Reiki time and time again. On reflection it was almost as if Reiki had chosen me. It was like the Universe was saying "okay, now it's your turn".

I attended my Reiki first degree course along with three others in Leicestershire, England. I must admit that I was very sceptical. I had read the pre-course work as requested and as the day progressed I waited with anticipation for my empowerments. As the teacher stood over me I felt an overwhelming sense of peace, love and tranquillity. Everything felt just right and I was brought to tears by how beautiful the whole process was. I felt similar on the other 2 empowerments that I received and I left to drive home feeling as if I was floating on air.

The following day I felt exhausted, I felt that I had not slept in weeks. I drank lots of water as suggested by my teacher. A few days later I began to physically clear out items from my house that I did not want or need. I felt a sense of inner calm and peace and, as I walked through the fields with my dogs, everything around me seemed to be brighter and more vibrant. It was as if someone had turned up the brightness on the television.

In the weeks and months that followed I began to notice a significant difference. I was more relaxed and calm. In situations where I would previously have become anxious, for example if a train was running late and as a consequence I would be late for work, I was relaxed. I always felt that everything would be okay. It felt as if some higher force, some higher being was looking out for like, like a guardian angel.

I also paid attention to the Reiki precepts. I initially reminded myself of them each day and then found that they were always in my consciousness. I began to worry less and I paid attention to my behaviour instead of criticizing others. I began to feel more empathy for people. At times if I was treated in a less than courteous manner, for example in a shop, then instead of complaining I was able to let things go. I began to put myself in the position of the other person. Perhaps the person was feeling unwell, or they may have recently suffered a death in the family, or something else. By doing this I felt better within myself. Naturally at times it is and was necessary for me to assert myself, but what I am talking about here are the small day to day niggles that seem to consume many people. People often say that their day is ruined by a minor event when the reality is that it is only that short period of time which may have caused some inconvenience. I began to remind myself that the past is history and that each moment can bring about a new beginning.

Needless to say, a few months later I signed up for my second degree. I began to work with the 2 energies: Cho-ku-rei and sei-he-ki. I found it fascinating that I could channel and change these energies simply by focusing my mind on them. I also began to meditate more and a feeling of inner calm became part of me.

I began working on family, friends and with clients. At the time of writing, I am currently renting a room above a health food shop locally in Leicestershire and a room in a beauty salon in Sutton Coldfield, West Midlands. I was and am truly amazed by the changes that I see in my clients. Many have experienced physical challenges, some psychological difficulties. The stories of their experiences leave me humbled and it is a pleasure to work with them.

I began working with my husband shortly after he was diagnosed with a rare type of muscular dystrophy and type 2 associated respiratory failure. At first I think that he only allowed me to work on him so that I could obtain some practical experience. After the first couple of sessions he began to feel better and more relaxed. As time progressed there were visible differences in his health. He is now able to walk a little better and further than the few short steps he could manage on discharge from hospital. He has less bad or off days and he has learnt to relax and pace himself. When he was initially diagnosed he was told that his condition was progressive and that he would end up in a wheelchair around 2 years later. He believes that the Reiki has helped him and continues to do so. He has regular sessions, almost daily ones, which he now looks forward to.

After working with clients for a while I signed up for the Reiki master course. I remember looking at the coursework and thinking that I would never remember all that I was required to. There were a few reasons that I signed up for this course. Firstly, a growing number of my clients were asking if I could teach them how to work with the energy. Secondly, I was curious: what would the master level teach me? Finally, I wanted to complete all three levels as I wanted to learn the whole process.

I recall receiving my master empowerments. My ability to work with the energies increased. I learnt to chant the sacred sounds and I seemed so much more connected with nature and with other people from the onset.

I began teaching others and at the time of writing I still do this. I love entering my student's world for a short while. Finding out about them, as much as they are willing to share, and introducing them to the energy. I especially enjoy attuning people to the first degree .When we carry out practical work and students experience the energy for the first time I enjoy the look of joy on their faces as they realise that yes, they CAN do it.

REIKI ESSENTIALS

Including:

- The Meaning of the Word Reiki

- The History of Reiki

- The Reiki Precepts

- And More ...

WHAT DOES THE WORD "REIKI" MEAN?

The Japanese word Reiki can be divided in to 2 parts: "Rei", pronounced "ray", means universal and "Ki", pronounced "key" means energy. The most popular translation therefore is that Reiki means universal life energy. There are other translations such as spiritual energy and soul energy.

Now that you are aware of the translation of the word "Reiki" from Japanese in to English no doubt you are probably even more confused. What does universal life energy mean and where does it come from?

Energy is all around us. Each person, plant and animal has an electromagnetic life force around them. Objects also carry vibrations. Each one of us is able to use this life energy to help ourselves and others on many levels. When a person studies a Reiki course, either in person or distantly, they receive a connection to Reiki by a specific ritual. Once this connection has been carried out that person is able to transmit Reiki for the rest of their lives. The more they work with the energy the greater their ability will be. Some people choose to move on through all three levels others are satisfied after completing their first or second degree. It is entirely up to you how far you wish to go. Think of the ability to work with Reiki like attending the gym. The more you practice the easier the exercises will be.

The next part of the question is: Where does Reiki come from? Well, as I have already mentioned, energy is all around us but where that energy comes from is a different question and to be honest nobody really knows. Some people say that it is healing energy from God. Now, who you believe God to be may be different from the beliefs of your next door neighbour. Perhaps you do not believe in God at all but have experienced Reiki for yourself, know that it is very real and offer another explanation as to where it comes from.

Another point of view is that when a person is connected to the Reiki source they are really connecting with themselves. What this really means is that the Reiki ritual which your teacher or master carries out is really connecting you to a part of yourself which has been lying dormant. Once a person receives this connection they often feel more in tune with their own life path. At times individuals have made dramatic life changes over a short period of time after being connected to Reiki. I believe that such changes are most common in individuals who are willing to work with the energy on a regular basis and are so far away from their life path that changes become noticeable quite quickly. Once connected to Reiki people often feel more in tune with both themselves and others. It is almost as if they are on a different level, perhaps on a different frequency. Solutions to problems come easier and life seems to flow better.

WHY DO PEOPLE LEARN REIKI?

There are many reasons why people learn Reiki, but there are a number of reasons which appear to be common amongst my students:

- A desire to feel better by reducing stress or anxiety.

- A need to feel more connected to themselves, nature and others.

- To improve health and general well-being.

- Because a friend has already learnt and has suggested that it may be beneficial.

- A feeling that something is missing in life.

WHO LEARNS REIKI?

Anyone can learn Reiki no matter what their age. I know of a person who empowered her 9 year old son and I have taught people ranging in age from 20 to 70. It does not matter what your age it is your desire to work with the energy that is important. Your occupation is also unimportant. I have taught people whose work ranges from: sales assistant, nurse, vet, doctor, scientist, teacher, mechanic, housewife, herbalist, sports injury massage therapist, secretary and many others.

Please remember that your job is not who you are, your job is only part of you and does not define you on a spiritual level. Reiki is for everyone. If we all learnt Reiki I truly believe that the world would be a better place. Reiki can also be learnt by people from all religious backgrounds. It really does not matter if you have deeply religious beliefs or none at all.

THE HISTORY OF REIKI

On the 15th August 1865 a baby boy was born in a small village in Japan. The boy was called Mikao Usui and, although he was born into a very poor and humble background, he would later create a system of healing which would touch the lives of many throughout the world.

As the boy developed he showed a keen interest in studying. It was said that he read whenever and whatever he could lay his hands on. His sharp mind and quick wit ensured that he was not taken advantage of and he could turn his hand to almost any task required of him. Usui was especially interested in religion and medicine and he had acquired friends with similar interests.

During his working life Usui was fortunate enough to gain a position as a public servant. This particular job involved a great deal of travel and Usui is said to have visited Europe, China and the USA. I can only imagine how exciting and interesting this must have been for him. Remember that, at this time, travel was uncommon and Usui would have looked physically different from those he encountered in foreign lands. This must have resulted in people staring at him and in return he must have thought that those other people looked very different from him too! Naturally the food and customs would have held a great fascination for him as would the way that illness was treated. Usui would have observed and studied and taken all of this information in and stored it in his keen mind for use later.

At some point, it is uncertain exactly when, Usui entered a Buddhist monastery. Usui was said to have been a keen student of Buddhism and was eager to discover the purpose of life. He found a Zen Buddhist who was willing to teach him. The meditations he carried out are at the heart of the Buddhist practice. The teacher would pose a question to his student and the student would meditate on this question and arrive at an answer. Not all questions required deep thought. The primary aim of this meditation was to focus the mind in the present. It is important to sit still and to be silent and in doing so you will increase your awareness of your environment and the sounds and sensations as they occur around you. Usui found however, that although these mediations were beneficial they did not lead him to discover the purpose of life. Usui felt compelled to discover his life purpose and there are a number of different stories which are told which attempt to offer an explanation as to how this happened:

- Usui discovered Reiki from hidden scrolls which were buried in the ground when he sat down to meditate.

- Reiki was discovered when Usui attended a 21 day Buddhist training course.

- Reiki symbols were "given" to Usui during a moment of enlightenment whilst he was fasting for 21 days at Mount Kurama.

It is highly unlikely that any of the above explanations are correct. Usui was a dedicated student of many subjects and it is highly probable that Reiki was discovered through many hours of research, meditation and self- discovery. Usui had important friends, many of which were highly respected and educated people and it is more likely that his system of healing was created through the sharing of ideas and support and encouragement of his peers.

Now that Usui had a system that would help heal people he began his healing clinic. Very quickly he became established and he found that people would travel from great distances to see him. Some of those that he healed as well as healers and people who became interested in healing asked him if he would show them how to heal and help others. It is important to remember that Usui did not call his system Reiki. In fact, we are really uncertain as to who first used this name. Usui did not call his system anything in particular at all.

The teaching was split into three levels:

The first Level/ Degree, also known as Shoden: This is the student's introduction to the energy. The student begins to work on themselves and they begin to work on family and friends. Usui was said to have taught each student differently. He would ask them to carry out tasks which included meditations and energy exercises. He would offer a problem and ask the student to suggest a solution. The possible solution would not be expected immediately. This was something that the student would be expected to meditate on with the answer developing over time.

Usui taught all of his students simple life rules to follow; these are known as the Reiki Precepts. He also taught the concept of mindfulness; he thought that it was essential that the student live in the here and now. Living in the present removes many of the stresses and strains of life .The healthier a person is, the better their connection to the Reiki source. The individual is then better able to understand themselves on a deeper level and if working on others they are better able to channel Reiki.

The Second level/Degree, also known as Okuden: If and when Usui thought that the student was ready he would then introduce them to the second level. Only a small percentage went from first to second degree. It was said that Mikao Usui was a perfectionist and he would have to be absolutely sure that the student was ready to move forward before taking them on to the second level. The student would learn to increase their connection to the environment. They would deepen their sense of oneness. Specific meditations were also introduced. The student would focus on really experiencing the energies so much that they would become one with them. The concept of distant healing was also introduced and students would be expected to become proficient in this method.

The Third Level/Degree, also known as Shinpiden or Master level: This is the final level of teaching. Very few students reached this level. Those that did would be expected to have a great understanding of themselves, who they really were on a spiritual level. A master was also expected to be proficient at distant healing.

The students would begin to chant the Kotodama. These sacred sounds have specific energies associated with them. They are said to originate from the ancient religion of Japan, Shintoism and the word Kotodama literally means "word spirit". This is based on the Japanese belief that when specific words are chanted they can elicit certain energies, these give off different vibrations depending on what is chanted and this aids healing.

Once a person was a master he would then become the student once more. The master would continually evolve and move along his or her life path. The master may become a student once more by studying another discipline. The master would not have mastered Reiki because Reiki can never be mastered. The energy works differently with different people and so our experiences are never the same. Those students that reached the master level may have studied for 2 to 3 years, and from the First to the Second degree level the student may have studied for 6 to 18 months. Remember, each person was seen as an individual and therefore some students took longer than others to move between the 3 levels. In fact, only a handful went on to become masters and there were only 50 to 100 who moved from first to second degree. This may have been because the teachings were difficult and it is said that Usui was difficult to please. Others may have moved away from the area or lost interest. Most of the students would have seen Usui weekly or daily for instructions.

As Usui continued his clinic and his teachings, Japan at this time was going through a period of rapid change. As Usui and his work continued he drew the attention of the Japanese military. One particular officer, Chujiro Hayashi was also a doctor and he was fascinated with Usui's healing methods. He also saw that these healing methods could be used by the soldiers so that they could help to heal themselves. At this time there was a chronic shortage of doctors.

Now Dr Hayashi was a Christian and he was not really interested in the spiritual side of Reiki. As you would have noted from reading the above, it took a long time to move between the different levels and most of the soldiers did not have the time or the inclination to carry out a vast number of meditations and the self- treatments. It is said that Usui would have been very much against war, however the military would have been very persuasive and Usui would have been told to show the officers how his system worked.

In order to quickly train the officers, Usui and his talented student Toshihiro Iguchi developed the Reiki symbols. There is some information which suggests that it was *only* Iguchi that developed the symbols. Whatever you believe, the symbols were created so that the students could quickly draw down 2 particular types of energy. It is unclear if the third symbol, which creates a state of oneness and is used in distant healing, would have been taught to the Christian students. These Reiki symbols are taught on my second degree course, along with their uses, and the symbols are generally taught on second degree levels wherever you look to study.

And so the officers, along with their symbols, went on their way and Dr Hayashi was said to have documented a series of hand positions that he found Usui was using when working with his patients. Dr Hayashi began to treat others using Usui's methods. One of his patients was called Mrs Hawayo Takata. She was from Hawaii and she was in Japan visiting her family after the death of her husband followed a short illness. Her sister had also passed on. She had travelled to Japan with her two daughters to inform her parents of the deaths. There are various stories which offer explanations as to how and why Mrs Takata became interested in Reiki; some say that:

- She was experiencing abdominal pains as a result of nervous exhaustion.

- She had a brain tumour and as she was being prepared for the surgery she heard a voice telling her to have Reiki.

- She had a vision that Reiki would make her well as she had a form of lung disease.

Well, once again it does not really matter which version you believe because what is important is that Mrs Takata played the main role in bringing Reiki to the Western world. Once she was cured of whatever illness or disease she had presented with, Mrs Takata become interested in learning the system that had helped her. She was taught all three levels by Dr Hayashi. She was the only woman besides his wife to become a Reiki master.

Mrs Takata begun to teach Reiki in Hawaii, however as she was aware that anything Japanese at this time would not be accepted to the US citizens she re-invented Miako Usui. The teaching changed so that Dr Usui was a Christian who had developed a method of healing others. Gone were the meditations and awareness exercises. Reiki became something that you had done to you. It became a treatment in the same way that aromatherapy and reflexology are. Mrs Takata also thought students should expect to pay vast amounts of money in order to become attuned to Reiki. In some cases it was said that Mrs Takata charged as much as it would cost to build a house. Usui, on the other hand, believed that it was only necessary to receive a gift. That gift may have been as simple as a piece of fruit if the person was of humble means. If they were wealthy however, the individual may have bestowed a much larger gift.

So, as you can see, Reiki has changed a great deal from the very humble origins of Mikao Usui. Mrs Takata attuned 22 Reiki masters. She made each one of them promise to teach Reiki the way that she had taught it and not to change anything. The original 22 then taught many other masters and their teachings spread throughout the USA, Europe and Australasia. Over time some of these teaching changed. Perhaps some changes came about as the original teachings were misunderstood. I also suspect that some teachers tried to improve the system by creating their own style and changing what had originally been taught. Sadly, we have lots of rituals with Reiki which are totally unnecessary. Below are 2 examples:

I had a student attend my second degree course after having taken the first degree elsewhere. She had been attuned to Reiki by bowing before the master who had dressed in a golden flowing robe. When I informed her that such a ritual was unnecessary she appeared to be very relieved.

Many courses do not provide any pre-course material. This is in the mistaken belief that the Reiki teachings must be kept a secret. I am not sure who this information should be kept from and why. There seems to be a particular pre-occupation with keeping the symbols secret. My second degree students have the pictures of the symbols in their manual. This is because I want the student to learn how to draw the symbols and be comfortable in doing to. One of the symbols is quite difficult to learn and requires a little time in order to get it right. On many Reiki courses the symbols are given to the students on pieces of paper during the course. The student is then expected to memorise the symbols and tear up the paper shortly afterwards. I am also aware of one particular course during which the student burns the drawing of the symbol in a sort of ritual.

Please note that I have not stated the above to mock or belittle other people's courses. It is simply to make you aware that these rituals or techniques are entirely unnecessary and that Reiki really is very, very simple.

After Usui's death a number of his original students formed the Gakkai or The Usui Memorial Society This was formed with the intention of keeping Reiki alive. Much of the more recent information regarding the history of Reiki has come from this society via other Reiki teachers. It is very difficult to establish contact with any of the members. Membership is only granted to those who have been recommended by fellow members. Some students have channelled their own symbols and appear to work with energy on different vibrational frequencies. When we reflect on the origins of Reiki we must be truly humbled by how Reiki has spread throughout the world and is continuing to do so. I believe that Reiki teachers and students are helping to make the world a more peaceful and better place.

EMPOWERMENTS OR ATTUNEMENTS?

When I was originally taught as a Reiki master I was shown how to attune and empower students. Over time, and with personal experience, I have found Reiju empowerments appear to be a much more powerful experience for the student, as well as being a beautiful process for the teacher to carry out.

So, what is the difference between an empowerment and an attunement, and is one really more preferable than the other?

Well, some schools only give attunements and this is because the teacher has only been taught Western style Reiki. Some teachers of Western Reiki state that an attunement is a way of directly connecting the person to the Reiki source. In other words it's sort of like plugging a person into the source.

Reiju, on the other hand, is seen by some as a more gradual and gentle approach. Reiju is seen as a process during which a person receives a spiritual blessing. The person receives this spiritual blessing from the teacher but it is ultimately from the source; wherever you believe that to be.

With both styles the student is opened up to the energy and this gives the student the opportunity to work on themselves on many levels.

There are many different ways that the teacher can attune and empower a student depending on how they were taught. It is important to state here that it is not necessary to become bogged down with trying to decide which style is best for you. In fact, some schools do not even mention which style of connection ritual they use. You may wonder why I have even mentioned it in this book. Well, as this book is about Reiki I believe that it is interesting for you to know as much about Reiki as you can. In addition, some courses may advertise that they offer Western style attunements or Reiju empowerments and when you come across these you will automatically know the difference.

THE 21 DAY REIKI CLEAR-OUT

After you have received your connection to Reiki many students are advised of a Reiki clear-out. My personal experience after my first degree was that I felt unusually tired on the day of the course and went to bed early. A few days later I was energised and began a physical clear-out of the old and unwanted items in my home. Below I have listed some of the ways that my students have experienced a clear-out:

Physical Clear-out

- Colds and flu like symptoms: These have been reported to be mostly mild in severity, although I did have one lady report that she was in bed for 2 days with these symptoms. It appears that the more that you need to remove or detox, the greater your symptoms will be.

- Mild aches and pains in limbs.

- A desire and need to drink lots of water, as if you are flushing toxins out.

- Headaches, usually mild in nature.

- A cessation of headaches in an individual who used to experience many.

- A strong desire to eat natural healthy foods.

Mental Clear-out

- A deeply relaxed mind.

- A reduction in mental clutter.

- The ability to see the complete picture and problem solve more easily

- Less negative thoughts

- A feeling that things will turn out alright in the end

- A deep feeling of mental relaxation.

- The ability to stay calm when those around you are not.

- A realisation and deep understanding of what the right path in life is for you.

Spiritual or Religious Clear-out

- The realisation that a particular religion is not right for you.

- A need to learn more about another religion

- The ability to question religious beliefs.

- A deep connection, love and compassion for all living things.

- An acceptance of others regardless of race and/or religion.

Many Reiki teachers advise the student to stay away from toxins such as alcohol, cigarettes and highly processed food for 21 days in order to carry out the clear-out. This is not necessary as your body will let go of the things that it does not need and that do not serve you. Naturally, it is better for your health if you can avoid such toxins anyway and if a person wishes to abstain from say alcohol for 21 days, there will additional and obvious health benefits. The choice really is down to the individual.

34

THE REIKI PRECEPTS

Usui gave his students a set of rules to live by; these are called the precepts, although some schools call them the concepts. There are a number of variations of the Reiki precepts and these variations will depend on the style of Reiki that your teacher was taught. So for example, if your teacher was taught Western/Takata style Reiki there may be changes to the precepts to reflect that. Those changes may include a statement such as "Honour God, your parents and teachers". Below I have written the Reiki precepts in the format that, at the present time of writing, I believe to be correct.

The secret method of inviting many blessings. The spiritual medicine for all illness:

For Today only:

- **Do not anger**

- **Do not worry**

- **Be humble**

- **Be honest with other people and in your work**

- **Be compassionate to yourself and others**

I personally find that these rules or precepts are suitable for all, no matter what the belief system. We will now look at each of the precepts individually. Usui advised his students to place their hands in the Gassho position, the prayer position, when saying the precepts.

For Today Only: This is not a precept as such but those three words are very important. The words act as a reminder for you to focus on the here and now. For today only literally means that. We cannot think too much about the past as it has gone and cannot be changed. We can change the way that we look at our past and heal ourselves but when we look at things or situations which may have happened in the past we are looking at them from the perspective, insight and knowledge of what has happened since then. We are really looking at things in the present. We cannot think too much about the future as the future is an illusion as things may not work out the way that we planned. We only have now, this moment and that is all that is guaranteed. Now I am not saying don't plan and have wishes and dreams. What I really mean to say is: remember that your life exists now and keep those good and bad things that are in your thoughts at the back of your mind or, better still, just let them go.

Do not anger: It is better for your physical and mental health if you do not get angry. Too much anger is destructive to you and your relationships. If you are an angry person you are really angry with yourself. Anger blinds us from the reality of the situation and we do not see things for what they really are but how we think they are. Our anger may be based on a similar situation which has happened in the past and not in the here and now. As anger is destructive to the individual and their relationships with others it is to be discouraged. Anger achieves nothing and affects the energy system in a negative way.

Do not worry: When we worry about things we tend to exaggerate and the situation, person or problem that we are worrying about seems so much bigger. There is a snowball effect. The more we worry the worse a situation seems to be, and the worse it appears to be the more we worry! We become caught up in a rollercoaster of negative emotions. If we can stop ourselves from worrying in the first place, then we see things how they really are and approach the situation accordingly. Worrying drains our energy and creative juices. Worrying depletes the energy system and contributes to dis-ease.

Be humble: Be modest. This is not to say that we can or should not accept when someone says "well done", or that we cannot accept or be pleased with ourselves when we have achieved something. In fact, some people are incapable of accepting praise or perhaps they feel that they are not good enough and when someone praises them they do not mean it. Such a person has problems with low self-esteem which needs to be addressed if they are to live a comfortable and happy life. Being humble is the ability and manner that a person accepts praise and other positive complements. Being humble means accepting complements gracefully and appreciating the words for what they are.

Be honest with other people and in your work: If we expect others to be honest with us then we must be honest to begin with. Being honest does not mean that you use cruel or spiteful words. Being honest means that you choose your words carefully and that you say what is necessary in a neutral way. Be honest in your work whenever you do a paid job of employment or any job at home or in the work environment, do it to the best of your ability. There are no shortcuts. When you carry out honest work you feel good about yourself. You feel proud and have a sense of achievement. This is good for your energy system as all of this positivity transmits positive vibrations throughout your whole body.

Be compassionate to yourself and others: Being compassionate means the ability to have the deep awareness and sympathy for the suffering of others and the desire to do something about it. Many people are able to be compassionate to others but they fail to be compassionate to themselves. It is really, really important to be compassionate to yourself. If you do not do this you are liable to make yourself ill and your body is likely to suffer. Many of us push ourselves too hard and fail to notice the detrimental effects we are experiencing until it is too late. Being compassionate to yourself may be as simple as giving yourself the gift of time each day. You may decide that what you really need is a few minutes each day to read a book or magazine that holds your interest. Even though this may appear to be a small gesture, this small gift of time has a big impact. What you are really saying is "I am an important person, I am kind to myself". Small acts of kindness to yourself will in turn increase your ability to be compassionate to all of mankind. With time, being compassionate to yourself by not taking on too much, getting rest when you are tired and saying no instead of yes when you really are unable to do something, will lead you down the path of a more fulfilled and healthy life.

Practical Exercise

I would like you to carry out this small exercise to help you increase your self-awareness:

- Begin by finding a quiet place where you will not be disturbed.

- Ensure that your feet are on the ground and that your hands are facing palms upwards and resting on your thighs.

- Now take a deep breath in through your nose. Now out through your mouth.

- If you are carrying out this exercise in the morning I want you to focus on yesterday's events. If you are carrying out this exercise at the end of the day then I want you to think about today's events.

- Think about the day and notice any emotions which are brought to the surface.

- Do you feel angry? If so why and what caused the anger.

- Are you worried? What are you really worried about. Was it the worry that caused the anger?

- Did you conduct yourself in a humble way with all that you encountered or did you display traits of arrogance or hostility which may have been a way for you to mask another emotion such as anger or fear?

- Were you honest with other people and with yourself? Were you honest with your family, friends and co-workers? If not why was this? Was it because you did not wish to hurt another's feelings or even your own? Was it easy not to be honest as this made life easier for you? Would you be happy if someone was less than honest with you?

- Were you compassionate to yourself and other people? Are you often criticizing yourself in your mind? Did you display compassion to another person when they were in need? If not was this due to fear – are you afraid that if you show compassion that others will think that you are weak or are you afraid that you may end up in the same situation if you are not too careful ? When was the last time that you were kind to yourself?

- Now make a note of all of the emotions that you would like to let go of.

- Now feel and/or see the emotions just drift way.

- Down your body, starting at your heart or your head (whichever seems to be the most appropriate).

- The emotions may appear as a black or grey cloud or as a thick fog or heavy rain fall.

- The negative emotions just drift away from your body and into the earth.

Now you have a better understanding of yourself and your behaviour and emotional responses. You can make the changes that you feel you need to. You may decide that you are feeling too much anger or that you are worrying too much. You may need to show compassion towards yourself.

Please try and carry out this exercise on a regular basis, noting down how you feel each time. You may decide to carry out this exercise only when you feel it is necessary. You choose. Whatever you decide it is your journey and your life.

The exercise that you have just done has created an increased awareness of your emotions, and you are now more aware of your reactions to those emotions. It may be wise to familiarise yourself with the Reiki precepts so that you can become more fully familiar with them; this familiarity will help to make permanent changes for the better. Some choose to read the precepts each day, mornings are often best as the reading/and or saying of the words out loud helps conscious awareness.

ENERGY, THE AURA & THE HUMAN BODY

Perhaps you are already a spiritual, psychic/ clairvoyant person. Perhaps the Reiki course that you have been on, or are going to attend, has opened up a whole new world for you. You now see things in a different way; you realise that we are more than our physical bodies.

As humans we are extremely intuitive. We often have gut feelings which we choose to ignore because these feelings are not really based on facts. If we have grown up in the west we have been taught that we focus primarily on the facts and what is presented before us. We make decisions based on facts and are discouraged from making decisions from the heart.

However, our intuition and emotions are always in the background, always present. We know intuitively when someone is walking too closely behind us. We may have feelings of negativity, fear or dread when thinking about taking a short-cut when walking home in the dark. Your intuitive side is always telling you something and it is up to you to listen and take any necessary action.

The human body, from an alternative point of view, is made up of the aura. There are also chakras and energy pathways that supply both the physical and subtle bodies with energy. When the majority of people talk about the aura it seems that there is a misunderstanding that the aura is just one layer of energy around the body; this is incorrect, the aura is made up of several layers:

The Etheric Body: This is the layer which is closest to the physical body.

The Emotional Body: Our feelings, thoughts and emotions are found in this area.

The Mental Body: Rational thoughts, values and emotions are represented in this layer of the aura.

The Astral Body: This layer acts as bridge between the physical and mental plane. This layer represents unconditional love for people, the environment, animals and plants.

The Etheric Temple: The ability to communicate and how our higher-self connects with the spiritual plane.

The intuitive Body: Our intuitive thoughts, feelings and emotions are found here.

The Causal Body: Our spiritual side, divine knowledge .This is where our higher-self lives.

When we begin to work with Reiki, and we learn to scan the body, we often find that there are areas of hot and cold. Illness is caused by a disturbance in the flow of energy. Most illness and dis–ease occurs over time: tiny holes appear in the aura to begin with and as the condition gets worse the hole in the aura becomes bigger and bigger. Negative energy affects the aura by working its way through the layers until it reaches the physical body. The person becomes symptomatic of an illness, presents to a medical doctor and they are given a diagnosis. Naturally, there are times when the body is involved in a physical trauma such as a car accident. In these types of cases the physical body is immediately affected, the aura is damaged and work must be carried out to repair at a physical level to begin with.

Karmic blockages can be felt in the aura. A Karmic blockage feels heavy, dense and thick. The blockage is attached to the soul of the person. If you talk to the person, who has the blockage, about their life they will talk about the pain (physical or emotional) that they feel and, as they continue to tell you about themselves, you will notice that they have been repeating certain types of behaviour (usually unconsciously) as if to serve and feed the blockage.

A Karmic blockage can appear as a ball or nut stuck in the aura. Some therapists are not able to see these blockages but they sense them instead. Most people believe that the word *Karma* means that if you do something bad to someone else then bad things will happen to you. Now, you may or may not agree with this statement, and it is entirely your decision to make either way. In Reiki, and other energy work, a person's life experiences can be stored in the aura if they have not dealt with a problem, or learnt from a previous mistake. If you believe in past lives the mistake could have been from a previous life. This karmic blockage is full of negative energy; draining and blocking the flow of energy around the body.

Once the problem has been addressed the blockage will be removed and the person will become well again. When the blockage has been removed the person will often state that they feel free, lighter and that everything flows. Karmic blockages can originate from any problem in life such as money, relationships and addictions such as alcohol, drugs, gambling and food. In fact the list is as long as the list of problems which have ever been known to mankind.

The more intuitive and sensitive we become the more we see what is really around us. We begin to see that the Universe is presenting us with solutions to our problems. Most of the time we choose to ignore the help we are offered and choose a different path. With Reiki we learn to really see what is around us and begin to pay attention to the messages we receive.

Energy is directed by the mind; what we think becomes our reality. In fact, there is no other reality than that which we ourselves create. This can be explained by an example: If you have gift of mobility and you can walk, imagine that you are walking down a street; you suddenly see a large dog that you do not know running towards you. If you love dogs you might look forward to greeting the dog. If you are afraid of dogs you might feel physically sick and dizzy, convinced that you are about be attacked. The dog begins to bark and if you are afraid you may think that it is getting ready to attack you. If you like dogs you may think that the 'woof' sound it is making is a form of greeting.

Our minds are constantly looking to make sense of our environment. We base our decisions not on reality but on our perception of reality. This is where our problems exist. Healthy people look at problems and situations in a positive way and expect most things to turn out okay. When we begin to think in a negative way we begin to supress our immune system. This allows negative energy to be attracted to the aura. The negative energy attracts more of the same like a magnet and pretty soon the person begins to become symptomatic of illness as the downward spiral begins. Reiki can work at removing the negative energy. This is why, after a treatment, people report feeling more relaxed and as if a weight has been taken off their shoulders. Reiki is guided by a higher power and it cannot do any harm.

Energy pathways supply both the physical body and the aura with vital energy. In India these subtle channels are called "Nadis"; this is an old Sanskrit word. There are 72,000 Nadis in the human body. The place where 2 or more Nadis cross over is called a Chakra. The major chakras of the body are: the Root, Sacral, Solar Plexus, Heart, Throat, Brow and the Crown. The Chakras take in energy from the aura, sucking it in like a spinning disc. Any energy blockages can lead to illness and disease.

In China energy pathways are called meridians. The meridians are essential to our understanding of Traditional Chinese medicine. Acupuncture, acupressure and pressure points are now techniques which we in the west are now familiar with. Yin and Yang create a constant state or flow of energy. Aura photographs easily show changes in a person's aura when a photograph is taken followed by another a short time later. If a persons' mood (energy) has changed from the first to the second photograph, the colours of the aura will appear to be different.

Yin and Yang are terms which began to be used in ancient China. Yang is seen as a male energy; it is hot and represents heaven. Yin is a colder but softer energy; it is seen to represent the female and is connected to the earth. Yin and Yang work with the aim to balance all that is life. We cannot exist if our environment becomes too hot or too cold. There must be a balance in all things. Reiki, acupuncture and other energy work aims to balance a person's energy. Too much hot or cold in any one area can lead to illness. With time the Reiki worker is able to become sensitive to the energy and can feel areas of hot and cold, sensing and aiming to remove any blockages and thereby restoring good health.

There are also three other energy centres in the body. These are called the Dantian or Tanden. The energy centres are situated:

Just inside the area of the lower navel and is concerned with the cultivation of the life force. (The lower Tanden)

At the same level as the heart and is concerned with the internal organs and respiration. (The middle Tanden)

The third is situated near the area of the third eye and is concerned with spiritual growth. (The upper Tanden)

I believe that it is important to have an understanding of the subtle energy systems of the body. However, we as Reiki teachers and practitioners are only concerned with letting the Reiki flow. The aim is to be neutral and to simply let the energy flow, safe in the knowledge that the energy is working for the highest good of the recipient.

YOUR MIND & REIKI

Including:

- Buddhism & Reiki

- Meditation

- Mindfulness

HOW TO WORK THROUGH THIS SECTION

I have enclosed the section on Buddhism & Reiki for information only so you may or may not decide to read this section.

The section on Meditation should be read and the exercises followed through.

Follow this with the section on Mindfulness. This contains a 4 weeks beginner's programme.

BUDDHISM & REIKI

Mikao Usui was a Tendai Buddhist monk. I have included a section on Buddhism in this book as it may help you understand how Reiki can be connected with Buddhism and how some of the ideas and concepts of Reiki may have evolved.

The Buddha's teachings were taken from India to Japan via China and Vietnam. It was in the 1950's and 1960's that Buddhism began to become popular in the West. It has been said that the Buddha was one of the world's most inspirational teachers. The Buddha was born Siddhartha Gautama. We are still uncertain as to when he was born although it is generally accepted that he born between 563 to 483 BCE in what is presently called Nepal. His parents were a king and queen and he wanted for nothing and lived in peace and harmony in the foothills of the Himalayas. It is said that the boy's mother died when he was young and he grew up being lavished with love, possessions and attention from his many relatives. The palace was full of healthy young people and the boy did not venture outside of its walls. One day, the curious Siddhartha begged his father to let him see what was on the other side of the walls. Reluctantly his father agreed. The streets were cleaned and all of the old, sick and infirm were removed. Riding with his guard, the young boy saw a sick and elderly man lying on the side of the road.

He must have been missed thought the guard and immediately requested that someone remove him from sight. Upon his return to the palace Siddhartha began to ask himself questions. What is the point in having riches and luxury if we are all going to get sick, old and die? Siddhartha then began to leave the palace on a regular basis and he saw others who were sick and infirm, as well as dead people. One day, feeling very dissatisfied, he simply got off his horse and sent the guard back to the palace asking him to tell his family that he would not return. The young Siddhartha cut his hair and began to live amongst the people. Siddhartha began searching for the meaning of life. He talked with many people and he learnt a great deal from their life experiences but he was looking for something more, so he began to meditate. It was during one such meditation that he became enlightened. From that moment on, the Buddha as he became known, began his teachings.

The basic principle of Buddhism is the Three Fold Path. This is based on the following:

Ethics
Not harming yourself includes not using intoxicating substances. Not drinking, taking drugs or engaging in risk-taking behaviour. Harming others applies to people and animals as well. Do not harm any other living thing.

Meditation
Siddhartha was enlightened when he meditated. Therefore, the practice of meditation will lead

us to enlightenment. This will happen over time. Meditation it will also lead us to the solutions to our problems. Meditation is essential to living well.

Wisdom
This comes with fully understanding ourselves and others. If we are wise we are thoughtful and not willing or quick to judge others. If we are wise we gain insight. Those who are judgemental are really basing their opinion on their own life and experiences and not on the problem as it is presented to them

The Buddha's teachings are not religious and they are not based on any religious teachings and scriptures.

In order to follow the teachings well a person must have a strong belief that they will benefit in some way. This is common sense really, after all a person would not do something which they are not expecting to benefit from. They must also accept that they must commit to a regular practice of meditation and make time for this.

Many people in the West have a certain image of what it is like to undertake a structured Buddhist training course. The image is generally one of happy relaxed people sitting in robes in a beautiful monastery. This may be the case for some retreats and courses and in some parts of the world. For most, especially those who undertake Zen training, the opposite is true. It is not uncommon to meditate for several hours per day with only breaks at meal times and to use the toilet. If the Zen Master notices that your mind has wandered you will be quickly brought back to where you need to be by a smack with a flat wooden slat. It is believed that an untrained and undisciplined mind will lead to dissatisfaction until death. Only enlightenment can change this.

Meditation helps a person to live in the moment. An individual must be satisfied with what they have now. If a person is meditating, and they feel thirsty, it is not that they do not want to be thirsty that is the problem but rather they want something other than what they currently have. They are dissatisfied; unfortunately, being dissatisfied leads to dis-ease - the person is ill at ease with what they currently have. This is the gap between what you have and what you want.

The purpose of meditation for the Buddhist is to move beyond the gap between where you are and where you want to be. A person will always be in this state of wanting what they do not have unless they learn to control their minds and to let go of selfish attachments. Our responses and actions are based on our thoughts. We can learn to control our thoughts and our internal world and this will help us to live well.

Tendai Buddhism teachings are based on the Lotus Sutra; this is the foundation document for Tendai Buddhists. The way to salvation is to achieve

Buddhahood. The teachings of the document itself were translated from Sanskrit to Chinese in 225 CE. This was the earliest historical documentation of its existence. The original text has been lost.

A sutra is a sermon and the actual words of the Buddha or those of his disciples are said to be what has been recorded.

A sutra is divided into many chapters. Everyone can reach a state of enlightenment by listening to these sermons as well as by their own actions and these actions include meditation. Compassion and the wish for others to be enlightened may also lead to a state of enlightenment.

However, it is important to remember that teachings alone are not enough: faith and devotion are also important.

In order to emphasise the importance of the role of faith and devotion, parables can be found in the Lotus Sutra. Here are 2 examples:

The Prodigal Son
This parable tells of a son who is very poor but who comes to realise that he has all that is important to him and that he is ultimately wealthy.

The Phantom City
A man has to lead a number of poor people on a difficult journey. The man creates an illusion of a beautiful and safe city that those who are travelling

with him keep in their hearts. This gives them the strength to carry on and it makes the journey appear easier.

Now that you know a little about Buddhism perhaps you can see how we can connect this with Reiki:

- Usui wished to achieve his own enlightenment. Perhaps this happened when he was meditating or perhaps he was a diligent student of healing and his methods developed over time and with practice.

- Perhaps Usui had discovered his personal path earlier than we originally thought and he was driven to show others how they could find theirs.

- When a person studies Reiki first degree they are introduced to the energy.

- Students must also work on themselves as well as working on others.

- When we work on ourselves it could be said that we are working towards our own enlightenment through self-healing and meditation.

- When working on others we are showing compassion and caring for another human being or animal.

MEDITATION

Whilst many people like the idea of meditating, and would like to feel more relaxed and calm, few apply themselves sufficiently to experience lasting, long term benefits. There are many reasons for this. It could be some expect instant results, perhaps some are unable (unwilling) to commit to a regular practice. I believe that for most, who really do set out with good intentions, they try to do too much too quickly. I myself, in the past, have bought specific CD'S and read books that have led me into a 60 minute daily practice straight away. Then guess what happens? For the first few days I manage to achieve my goal and then life gets in the way and my time is consumed with other things which appear to be more important than doing what I used to perceive as just sitting there. That was my initial experience and impression of meditation. I am so glad that I discovered that I was wrong.

After I attended my Reiki first degree course, and I began to carry out the specific meditations that had been shown to me on a daily basis (more on these later), I began to feel the real benefits of meditation. This in turn got me thinking: why do people try to meditate for long periods of time to begin with? After all, if I wanted to get fit I would be foolish to try and run 10 miles on the first day of a fitness regime. So, I began to carry out my own meditations. I began with just 5 minutes each day. Yes just five minutes. You can start with less, like 2 minutes if you find 5 minutes difficult. I did carry out my Reiki meditations in addition and at a separate time. I did this because I really wanted to find out if I could meditate under my own guidance. I wanted to discover if I had the strength of mind and the willpower to do this.

So, now going back to the 5 minutes a day (or less). I think that anyone and everyone can manage to do this. In order to inspire or motivate you I have decided to list some of the benefits of meditation.

THE BENEFITS OF MEDITATION

To begin with, many people want to feel more relaxed and calm, to generally have a better quality of life. Other benefits include:

- An increased connection to the Reiki Source

- Lower blood pressure

- Decreased fat/lipid/cholesterol content in the blood.

- Reduced heart rate

- Improved circulation

- Clearer skin

- Brighter sparking eyes

- Reduced feelings of stress and anxiety

- Greater emotional stability

- Reduced dependency on alcohol, smoking, over eating or other self-destructive habits

- A better understanding of oneself

- Closer to God, the creator or the source

- Enlightenment

- Spiritual guidance

- Inner peace and generally feeling very, very calm

- Feeling brighter and generally more alert and aware of your environment

Now I am sure that there are 1 or 2 reasons on this list that have attracted your attention. Perhaps you can add a few personal reasons as well. I am sure that you now have an incentive to meditate.

WHAT IS THE DIFFERENCE BETWEEN RELAXATION & MEDITATION?

Now you may be thinking that you don't really need to meditate because you relax on a regular basis. You may go to the gym and be a really active person and feel great for doing so. You may relax by sitting in front of the television and you enjoy watching a great movie. You feel the benefits of relaxing. Your mind wanders. You let go and you may even feel any tension in the back, neck and shoulders just disappear as you relax. All of this is great. When you relax you do not think of anything and your mind drifts and flits from one thing to another back and forth. This is relaxation.

Meditation is different because it requires effort. Whilst it may be argued that progressive relaxation exercises require effort, meditation is different. Meditation leads to a deep state of awareness by continual and sustained focus. This focus may be on:

- An object such as a candle

- An affirmation, word or mantra

- A focus on your breathing

- Visualisation exercises

When a person meditates they are told to focus their attention and to let everything else go. If the mind does wander you must make the effort and bring yourself back to your primary focus.

When a person meditates, activity in the brain changes. There are 4 different types of brainwaves:

Alpha Waves: These are most prominent when we want to relax and slow down. They are connected to the creative aspect of ourselves. This could explain why artists, musicians and writers often appear to be relaxed and chilled out as these brainwaves are highly dominant in their working lives.

Beta Waves: These waves relate to our normal state or level of consciousness. They represent the conscious part of ourselves and are connected to concentration and logic.

Theta Waves: These brainwaves are dominant when we are problem solving.

Delta Waves: These brainwaves relate to our state of deep sleep. We are still aware during sleep, but our subconscious mind is dominant.

During meditation there is a combination of alpha and theta waves. There is a synthesis of the conscious and subconscious mind. It is often during or after meditation that a person may find a solution to a problem that has been bothering them. If someone meditates on a regular basis problem solving will become easier and they will know the path that is right for them. So, now before you begin your own journey I want you to consider the following points:

There are 2 specific exercises that you will need to carry out in order to make your Reiki stronger and to deepen your connection to the Source. These are:

Hatsurei Ho

And

The Self- treatment meditation

Both of which are explained later in this book, I mention these now because these will require some of your time on a daily basis. It is a good idea to establish when in the day you are able to carry out these meditations. Be honest with yourself. It is no good trying to rush through these mediations and then race in order to get ready for work. If you can manage to comfortably get up around half an hour earlier then that's great but you do not want to defeat the object of achieving a state of calmness and then rushing through your day. Many people find that they have a little more time in the evenings and set aside 15 to 30 minutes to carry out the Hatsurei Ho exercises and/or the self-treatment meditation and then begin their own practice.

Decide How Long To Meditate
As most people lead busy lives, you need to organise your time well. Failure to do so will lead to frustration and disappointment and you not receive the many benefits that meditation can offer. You may carry out the specific meditations connected to Reiki and you may then decide to meditate yourself for an additional 5 minutes to begin with.

Decide On Your Style of Meditation
Choose a style which is most suited to you. You know yourself better than anyone. Are you best suited to:

Focusing on an object such as a candle: You may love a particular fragrance which may be associated with pleasant memories and choose to use that particular type of candle.

You may find it best that you **focus on a short word** such as :

"OM" or *"Aum"*

You may choose your own words. If you do this try to keep it simple such as

"I am calm and peaceful".

For the more adventurous amongst you, you may choose to use the Hare Krishna Mantra. The mantra is composed of just 3 words. These words are:

Hare Krishna Rama

Hare means to take away. When this word is chanted it is asking for God to take away pain, sorrow and negative feelings.

Krishna & Rama are both avatars of the Lord Vishnu. An avatar in Hindu terms is a descendent of a God in another form. Lord Vishnu is said to have descended the earth in order to establish law and righteousness.

The words of the Hare Krishna prayer are as follows:

Hare Krishna, Hare Krishna, Krishna, Krishna, Hare, Hare

Hare Rama, Hare Rama, Rama, Rama, Hare, Hare

When these words are chanted it is best to keep their meaning in your mind. The meaning therefore, is that you are asking for the Gods to take away your pain and discomfort.

Why not try it and see what happens?

Focus On Your Breathing: You may find that you can meditate best by carrying out deep breathing exercises. You must ensure that you do not over breath as you may feel a little dizzy. The purpose of concentrating on your breathing is to concentrate your focus inwardly and to slow down your thought processes.

Meditate By Visualisation Exercises: This may be best if you have a particular goal in mind. You can visualise how you want to look or act. Visualise yourself getting that job you really want or visualise peace of mind by allowing your mind to go to your own secret place of inner calm and peace. Naturally it is best if you are a visual person and can manage to see things in this way easily.

Okay, now you may have decided the best style of meditation for you. A little further on in this chapter I have included some meditations for you to try out.

Decide Where to Meditate
You must find somewhere which is going to be your healing space. It could be somewhere you will carry out your Reiki treatments. If you are lucky you may have a specific room or area dedicated to this. If this is not possible for you at this time, choose a place in your home where you will not be disturbed. Ensure that you turn off all telephones (remember the house telephone as well as your mobile).

If there are other people living in the household with you please tell them that you are going to be carrying out meditation exercises on a daily basis at a specific time and request that you are not disturbed for this short time. Some family members are great at respecting this, others really are not and find it difficult to respect your privacy. If the latter is your household, then simple ignore any unnecessary disturbances. It is amazing how quickly people catch on that you mean business and that it is not a good idea to disturb you. If you live in a household with small children, and really do struggle to find a quiet time to carry out your meditations, perhaps you can carry out the meditations once the children have gone to bed. If you share the responsibility with someone else it may be wise to meditate when they are at home so that you can have your quality time.

Try to set the scene by using scented candles, playing music, drawing the curtains or even hanging up suitable relaxing, calming, pictures or posters. Remember this is your time, do what is best suited for you.

Now finally, before you get going, a word on posture. Now many people think that you need to sit in a specific position in order to meditate properly. Many have been taught that they need to sit with legs crossed in the Lotus position in order for meditation to work. This really is not true. You must relax and be comfortable. If you practice Yoga on a regular basis or have hypermobile joints you may find it extremely comfortable to sit on the floor crossed legged. Most people do not. Many choose to sit on a chair (with or without arms). Please ensure that you are not slumped as this blocks the flow of energy. You do not need to sit ram rod straight either. Just sit up, legs uncrossed and feet flat on the floor. This ensures that oxygen gets to all of the muscles, you are not putting any strain on your joints and any excess energy goes back to the earth.

Before you begin any of the meditations listed below you may wish to monitor your progress. It may be wise to set a timer or an alarm so that you do not become bogged down timing yourself. Students often mention that they keep looking at a clock or watch in order to see if they have "done their time" in the early stages. This clearly defeats the purpose. Remember, meditation is ultimately about totally focussing and absorbing fully in the moment without distractions. However, this is the ultimate purpose. It is okay to be kind to yourself by setting a timer as mentioned earlier. Be careful however, you don't want any loud ticking noises which may distract you as a beginner.

If you monitor yourself you will know when you are ready to increase the number of minutes from say 2 to 4. You will know when you can do this when you find that you are not easily distracted and that you are able to return to focussing on your meditation easily if a distraction does occur.

You must also decide how long you are ultimately going to meditate for: are you aiming for 30 minutes a day or 60 minutes? Does your daily schedule allow for this amount of time? It is better to meditate for 30 minutes each day rather than for 60 minutes on alternate days. It may take you a few weeks or even months to reach your ultimate goal of meditating for a specific amount of time.

You will notice changes which will be subtle at first. You will also have to factor in time for your Reiki meditations. I cannot emphasis how important these are. Remember your personal meditations will help you develop strength of mind and this in turn will increase your ability to concentrate when carrying out self- healing or when working on others.

Basic Meditation: Focussing on an object

- Choose an object such as a flower, a candle or a picture.

- Close your eyes for a moment and concentrate inwardly.

- Open your eyes and look at the object.

- Focus on it. Notice the colour, shape and texture. If it is a picture imagine that you have shrunk down. You are a tiny, tiny person and you are in the picture.

- Remember focus, do not stare and remember to blink.

- If your attention wanders pull yourself back and concentrate on the object.

- When your time is up, close your eyes for a few seconds.

- Now open them.

- Slowly bring your awareness back to your environment.

Basic Meditation : Focusing on a word or mantra

During this meditation we will focus on AUM

- Begin by closing your eyes for a moment.

- Quiet your mind.

- Become aware of any part(s) of your body that is/are tense.

- Where you are holding tension just relax your body

- Let the tension go.

- Now, you can say AUM either silently or out loud.

A Few tips:

- Try to say the word at a pace that is just right for you.

- Try to keep the pace constant and not too fast.

- AUM should not sound too loud. It should appear to be in the background. It is just like having the radio on quietly at home.

- AUM will change your vibrational frequency and with practice will lead to a deep shift in your consciousness.

- Remember, if you become distracted bring your focus back.

When you are ready open your eyes. End the meditation by bringing your focus back on to the everyday sounds around you.

Basic Meditation: Focusing on your breathing

- Close your eyes and listen inwardly to the sound of your breathing.

- Focus inwardly and let go of any parts of your body that feel tense.

- Now, with your eyes closed inhale through your nose to a count of 4

- Hold – for a count of 2

- Exhale through your mouth for a count of 8

- Keep breathing in this way

As usual, if your mind wanders, bring your focus back to your breathing. Remember, you can always deal with a problem or anything that is bothering you later. Also remember that the solution to your problem may come to you after you have finished meditating.

Basic Meditation - Focusing on visualisation

Most people can visualise, but doing it well can take practice. The key to being good at it is to visualise a place that you like; this could be somewhere you would like to go, have already been or somewhere that is completely in your imagination. You choose. It is your experience.

- Begin by choosing what you are going to visualise. When I carry out this exercise I like to think of a tropical Island, somewhere like Hawaii, one of my favourite places. I choose a particular place and fill in the gaps in my memory to make it my own special place.

- Now close your eyes and see yourself in your own special place.

- Take your time to have a good look around.

- You may hear the waves of the sea or perhaps feel the sun warming your back, not too hot or not too cool.

- In your mind now turn up the brightness of the scene in front of you.

- Focus on what you see.

- Now, if your mind wanders bring your focus back.

- When you are ready you could imagine yourself taking a walk during your visualisation exercise.

- When you are ready, close your eyes and bring yourself back. Release the visualisation by allowing the picture to just fade away.

Good luck with your meditation practice. Next I have selected some of the most common questions that students who experience difficulty meditating ask. Hopefully your meditations will go well and you will quickly gain many benefits. If this is you, you may still want to refer to the next section but for reference only.

10 QUESTIONS & ANSWERS TO MEDITATION PROBLEMS

Can I meditate when angry?
Whilst meditation can help reduce anger, in the early stages of your practice it is best to meditate when you are calm and relaxed. If you feel angry often remember the Reiki precepts. Learn them and say them either silently or out loud before you begin your meditation and before you carry out the Hatsurei Ho or self-treatment meditations. Remember that anger is a destructive emotion. Take your time to learn the true source of your anger and deal with it.

I am unable to meditate for more than 5 minutes, I seem to be stuck, I feel a failure. My aim is to reach 15 minutes each day. Please help.
I am uncertain as to how you have tried to increase the duration of your meditations. Perhaps you have been increasing your time too quickly. Perhaps you are stuck because you are focusing on the time spent meditating. Learn to relax more and to let go. Try to ask yourself the reason why you are stuck. If you are honest with yourself it may be because you are afraid to go deeper. Try practicing the following exercise:

Before you begin your meditation close your eyes and say to yourself. I am now going to let go of all of my fear and other negative emotions. Imagine any and all negativity just drifting like grey rain drops, all the way down your body and to the earth. Open our eyes when you are ready and begin your meditation feeling refreshed and cleansed.

I find it difficult to stop fidgeting and to sit still.
You will not experience the benefits of meditation if you keep moving about. Remember – when you start to fidget bring your focus back and concentrate. Keep doing this as often as necessary to keep yourself on track. In addition, if you are really restless perhaps you need to look at how you are seated. Are you really comfortable and are you getting enough exercise?

My family will not support my practice and this makes me unhappy. Should I continue to meditate?
You must do what makes you happy. When you state that the family will not support you I am uncertain as to what this fully means. Perhaps your family have certain religious beliefs that conflict with the practice of meditation. If this is so, explain to them what meditation is and what it is not. Show them this book so that they can read and absorb all of the necessary information if they so choose. Continue your practice and gain the benefits. The more peaceful you become the less important other peoples' opinions will be to you.

I find it hard to be peaceful most of the time. Am I doing something wrong?
Well, first of all, do not be too hard on yourself. You have recognised when you are not peaceful. You do not like feeling this way and you want to take steps to experience a state of peace more often. Remember that we can control our inner world and this does require practice, this will come. We are unable to control our external world and what goes on all around us. Given time you will learn to let negative emotion just pass you by. This will not happen all of the time. Naturally it really depends on the situation. I can safely say that the more you "get into meditation", the more relaxed and calm your life will become.

I can't find anywhere quiet enough to meditate. What should I do?
We can all find somewhere to meditate if we look hard enough. This is not meant to be a harsh answer to your question, rather it is asking you the following: are you looking for somewhere totally silent in order to meditate? If this is the case you may never find anywhere without sound, noise or distractions. Given time you will learn to meditate with any distractions but I appreciate that for the beginner this is difficult. Remember – when your mind wanders bring your focus back. If you find this really, really hard, once a thought enters your head say to yourself (either out loud or silently) I will deal with this later.

I work shifts and my life is busy, I find it difficult to stick to a schedule.
If you work shifts or irregular patterns, plan at the beginning of your week when you are going spend time meditating and stick to it! For those who work shifts, your body clock has difficulty adjusting and therefore it is really important that you maintain a regular practice of meditation for your health.

What should I do with my hands during meditation?
You can do a number of things, the choice is yours really. You may:

- Put your hands in the prayer position.

- Place your hands on your lap, palms up.

- Hands on lap, palms down.

- Sit on your hands to prevent fidgeting and moving about.

When carrying out the specific Reiki meditations you will be guided as to where and how your hands should be positioned at all times.

Is age a barrier to meditation?
No. Life is a journey. Meditation helps bring things into focus and clears the mind. This benefits the young and the not so young as well.

When I go on holiday should I meditate?
This is an interesting one. If a person asks this question perhaps they are not enjoying their time spent meditating. With practice meditation will become part of your life and you will feel that something is not quite right if you miss out on your practice. After all, no one takes a holiday from carrying out life's little essential activities such as bathing.

STUDENT EXPERIENCES OF MEDITATIONS

"I have been carrying out meditation for 3 months now and I can safely say that I am now able to let go of all of the stress at work. I used to run things over and over in my mind and I feel so much better now that I have stopped this." (Andrew)

"I feel much more in control of my life now that I have been introduced to Reiki and to my meditations." (Lorraine)

"I am starting to teach all of my family to meditate. I feel so excited." (Sandy)

"I have a high-pressure job. Now that I meditate I can find solutions to problems easily and quickly." (Henry)

"When I meditate I go into another world. It feels like a mini-holiday that I go on every day" (Vanessa)

"Now that I have been meditating for 6 months I have found that I have been better at playing chess." (Paul)

"Meditation has helped me become a more compassionate person. I also remind myself of the Reiki precept before meditating, it helps me concentrate." (Sonya)

"Thank you for showing me how I can become a better person by slowing down. I now think before I speak – all due to meditation and Reiki." (Sarah)

"Meditation has helped me really see that there are no problems, only solutions." (Tony)

"Reiki and meditation has helped me become a grateful person. I feel gratitude each and every day. I give thanks that I am alive." (Zoe)

MINDFULNESS

The concept of mindfulness has become very popular in recent years. I recently received a business email from a colleague which proposed I was "mindful" of a specific situation. Mindfulness has become a fashionable word which people are currently using to suggest that the person to whom they are referring should be thoughtful of another person, situation or event; this is not really how mindfulness was or is supposed to be used. I have included this section as an introduction to mindfulness for 3 main reasons:

- Mikao Usui practiced mindfulness as well as teaching mindfulness to his Reiki students. If we are to keep as close to the original source as possible it is important for students now to understand these principles.

- Being mindful will increase your self-awareness which in turn will help you in your journey towards self-discovery/enlightenment.

- Stress and anxiety are common aspects of modern day living for many people. In order to live well we all need to keep stress and anxiety under control. Mindfulness can help to reduce or eliminate the symptoms of stress and anxiety.

The Buddha is considered to be the person who first introduced the concept of mindfulness - mindfulness is part of the Noble Eightfold Path. In the Western world it was Jon Kabat-Zinn who, in 1979 introduced the first Mindfulness-Based Stress Reduction Programme at the University of Massachusetts. It should be pointed out that mindfulness itself is not based on any religion or religious practice although the origins of mindfulness clearly derive from Buddhism.

One of the reasons why mindfulness has become so popular in recent years is really due to the Western lifestyle. For most of us the way we live is slowly killing us. Yes you read correctly, I wrote *killing us* and I do not write these words easily. Think about it for a moment. The pace of life has really escalated in recent years and for most of us we are constantly scrambling just to keep up. There is an increase in stress related mental health problems and heart problems as well as skin complaints such as eczema. The stress has to get out somewhere and why not via the skin? Now, take the average family; I am not sure if there is an "average family" now, but please humour me so that I can get my point across. Okay, the average family of 2 parents and 2 or 3 children. Both parents work, in many cases just to make ends meet. As well as working the children may have to be picked up and dropped off from school and sometimes more than one school, the home has to be looked after so there is cooking, cleaning and shopping to do as well as correspondence to reply to and bills to pay. The garden needs to be attended to and there may be parent evenings, groups and clubs to attend. In addition to this there is the telephone ringing, landline as well as mobile and emails to answer. When the family are at home at the end of the day there is no down time. Someone from work is always able to contact you and as a result of this you are not able to switch off and relax. By the time you have had your evening meal your mind is racing ahead to the next day. You begin to think of all of the things that you will have to do tomorrow and you begin to make lists in your head which you may go over and over again. Before you know it you are lying in bed and thinking that the evening has gone far too quickly. The next thing you are aware of is the alarm clock as it is time to wake up to another frantic day. Yes this is modern living.

Even if you are not the average family and you live alone or perhaps you are caring for elderly relatives I bet you can recognise yourself by the description you have just read. I am not saying that the solution is to throw away all of your gadgets and go and live a primitive life in a cave somewhere. No, I am suggesting that you continue to read this section of the book and practice the concepts that it introduces. This is because you can have more control over your mind and your life than you previously thought.

When I talk to people about mindfulness they simply believe that they just need to be live more in the present. Yes they say, that's a great idea. I will try and live in the here and now. Some believe that it simply means that they should live for today and in many ways they are right: the Reiki precepts do say "just for today". However, living just for today can lead to disaster if taken too literally. If a person does this they may find that they reach old age without becoming financially secure and feeling that life has just dragged them from one job or place to the next, their life ending up directionless and without purpose.

So, now you may be asking: WHAT IS MINDFULNESS?

The simplest way to explain mindfulness is to say that most of us live our lives in a cloud the majority of the time. We are thinking of other things people, places and so on and not living in the moment. This moment may be walking down the road, driving a car or ANYTHING ELSE. We always seem to want to be somewhere else or doing something else. The gap between where we are now and what we are thinking about or where we want to be is where the problem lies. This leads to a life which is lacking, leading to discontent and unhappiness and even illness. A mindfulness programme will show you how to live in the here and now and train you how to do so.

When carrying out this introduction to mindfulness you will be concentrating on:

- Becoming increasingly aware of your thoughts, feelings and environment

- Becoming more compassionate towards yourself and others

- Challenging yourself and making small changes in your life

- Carrying out specific meditations

When we become more aware of our thoughts we are able to slow down or stop negative thoughts from spiralling out of control. Sadly, this downward spiral happens too easily. Try this exercise:

Sit and think of something which recently made you feel sad. Think for one minute only and stop. Now write down all of things that went through your head and continue reading this book.

Now, I guess that you not only wrote down the first thing that made you feel sad but a whole string of other things as well. I asked a colleague to carry out this exercise and this is what she wrote;

Thought about a neighbour that had died - then thought about relatives that had died - thought about my own mortality and health related issues and began worrying about my own health - began to think about something I had heard on the local news about a car accident where someone had died.

Next I asked her to think of something that had made her feel very happy recently. Again carry out this exercise yourself. Think of something that made you happy for one minute only and stop. Then write down your thoughts and return to this book.

This is what my colleague wrote: *I thought of my holiday plans for this year which are to visit my sister in Australia - I then thought of all of the places we had discussed by email that we are going to visit - I then thought of warm weather, other holidays that I had been on and my mind seemed to focus on warm sunshine and beautiful beaches.*

As you can clearly see, I asked this lady to think of the first thing that made her sad and the first thing that made her happy. Note that her mind jumped from one thing to the next very quickly and all of this occurred in the space of one minute. See how uncontrolled her thoughts were? The majority of us are like this. We have little control of our thoughts and therefore as you can see, those thoughts become out of control. If we are not careful our thoughts end up controlling us. If we think too negatively it is easy to see how that negativity can take control of our lives. One negative thought runs into another and pretty soon the world can appear to be a harsh and negative place.

It is important for Reiki students to learn to take control of their thoughts and practice mindfulness. If they do not, how are they able to allow the Reiki energy to pass through them to their clients, family and friends and remain neutral in the process? How are they able to practice Reiki well?

My guess is that when you carried out the above exercise your thoughts also jumped from one to the other. Now that you have an increased awareness of how little control most us have over our thoughts.

This can be a frightening and worrying experience. Do not worry; all of this can change if you are willing to put the effort in and apply yourself. The results will be worth it.

You must also practice becoming more compassionate towards yourself and others. Compassion and the importance of it is mentioned elsewhere in this book, in particular with regard to the Reiki precepts. Please be aware that in order to live a life that is in the here and now you must be aware of what your body and mind are telling you. If you are tired you must rest. You will not be able to carry out Reiki treatments effectively or work on yourself if you are too tired to do so. Compassion walks hand in hand with empathy. By putting yourself in the position of another you are being less judgmental and increasing your understanding of others and the world around you, no matter what your age or experiences in life.

Mindfulness is also about making small changes which have the potential to give big results. Many of us live the majority of our lives on auto-pilot. This is because, for the majority of the time, little changes from day to day. We carry out the same tasks day in and day out. We live our life in our heads and in a fog and unless we experience something very different the days just blend into one. This is why many people say that the years have passed them by and that time has gone quickly. It is not that time itself has somehow speeded up but the fact is that the person cannot recall anything of significance, or few events of significance, to account for that time.

Reiki attunements, and/or empowerments, are there to help a person wake up, to help them become more in line with whom they really are and, by carrying out the self-treatment meditations and the Hatsurei Ho exercises, a person becomes more connected with who they are. Small changes which we make in our everyday lives can lead to bigger changes over a period of time.

It is essential to the concept of mindfulness that we become aware of what is around us. Perhaps you could begin by taking a walk through the park on your way home, by driving a different route home or by getting off the bus one stop earlier so that you can take in the sounds, sights and colours not through the glass barrier of the car or bus but by really seeing with your own eyes, perhaps for the first time.

There are also a number of meditations to help you get started including the Body Awareness Meditation.

Now it's time to begin your 4 week programme.

Each week you will be asked to carry out and 1 or 2 other exercises which will help you increase your mindfulness.

WEEK 1 MEDITATION

This meditation focuses on your breathing. When you focus in this way you are not thinking of anything else and you are living in the moment. Like the other meditations in this book if your mind begins to wander, as it surely will at first, bring your attention back to where your focus is, on your breathing, by releasing any thoughts or worries as you can deal with them later when you can give the object of your concerns your full attention.

Breathing Meditation

- Find a comfortable chair where you can sit down and place your feet flat on the ground.

- Inhale for a count of 6.

- Hold for a count of 2.

- Exhale for a count of 6.

- As you inhale let any feelings of stress, worry and anxiety go up your body. All the way up.

- Hold those feelings as you hold your breathing for a count of 2.

- And then let go.

- As you let go release those feelings.

- As you continue to exhale feel the stress and tension just disappear from the body.

Now repeat this exercise and keep doing so for 5 minutes.

At the end, close your eyes and become aware of any feelings and sensations in your body.

You are most likely to experience feelings of deep relaxation and contentment. Well done, you were focussing on the moment, really living in the here and now.

Tasks to Aid Mindfulness
When most of us are getting ready for the day we are thinking of other things. This week I want you to focus on:

The sensation of water on your skin as you shower or have a wash in the morning. Also focus on the fragrance of the shower gel or the soap or whatever cleansing medium you use.

After you have washed, focus on the sensation of your clothing as you get dressed. By focusing on these tasks at the beginning of the day you are training your mind to focus on the here and now.

If you need or want to think about the day ahead, perhaps you have several things you need to do and you have made a list that you want to check, or perhaps you have a meeting to attend or some directions to look at before you start out for the day, then that is okay. We all need to plan and sort out things in advance. It is essential that we all understand and accept that forward planning and reflection are necessary. You just need to ensure that you are living in the moment the majority of the time.

Continue this programme for 7 days. On the 7th day spend a few minutes reflecting: has this week gone the way you thought that it would have? What have you learnt this week and have the small changes you have made this week been beneficial?

WEEK 2

A little note: You may find that your mind wandered whilst carrying out the mindfulness meditation during week 1. Please do not become disheartened, remember that your mind is like a muscle and it needs to be trained. Remember, and keep reminding yourself if necessary, that you would not master a language, a skill or a form of physical exercise in 1 week so why would you be expected to master mindfulness in that short space of time?

The Body Awareness Meditation
This meditation is designed to concentrate your attention on your body and it will allow you to become aware of the subtle messages that your body is telling you.

Allow 15 to 20 minutes for this meditation.

- As usual, find a quiet place where you will not be disturbed and sit with your feet on the floor.

- Begin at the top of your head.

- Focus your attention at the crown and become aware of any thoughts and feelings in this area. Release any pain you may be feeling just by letting it go. Stay focused on each area as stated below for several minutes in turn.

- When you are ready, bring your attention to the front of your face. Again, become aware of any tension, feelings or other thoughts and sensations in this area. Remember to focus over the whole of the face: the eyes, nose and mouth as well as the jaw which holds a lot of tension when a person is feeling under stress. Again let go of any pain in this area.

- Now, in turn focus your attention on the following areas of your body, remembering to pay attention to thoughts feelings and sensations in each area in turn and to let go of any pain (physical or mental) that you feel:

- Focus on your throat.

- Your heart

- Your thighs

- Your feet including your toes

- When you have finished just allow any residual thoughts that you may have to just drift away from you and slowly allow your focus to return to the present

- Repeat The Body Awareness Meditation for 7 days

Tasks to Aid Mindfulness
Become more aware of your posture. This week I want you to notice the way that you sit and walk. Remember that you will feel and look better if you sit up that little bit more. Depressed people walk with their shoulders slumped and this in turn affects their breathing. There is reduced oxygen to the cells of the body, this in turn also affects their ability to think clearly and move easily.

If you are physically able to, take a short walk in your neighbourhood. A five or ten minute walk can be managed by even the busiest of people. As you walk, become aware of all that is around you. Live in the moment, concentrate on your posture and take deep breaths. When you arrive home make a note of how you feel.

WEEK 3

This week you are going to concentrate on observing your own thoughts actions and behaviours. This week is concerned with:

Negative or self - destructive habits
What are the thought processes are that lead you to repeat those habits?

The Mindfulness Relaxation Meditation
- With your feet flat on the floor sit in your special place for meditation.

- Close your eyes and take a deep breath in through your nose for a count of 4.

- Hold for a count of 2.

- And breathe out.

- As you breathe out I want you to say to yourself the words "LET GO".

- As you breathe out you are letting go of any stress and tension that you have been holding onto. This may be:

    - Mental stress and worry

- Physical tension in the muscles.

- Keep repeating this exercise for 5 minutes and then take one final deep breath in and as you exhale open your eyes and slowly allow your awareness to return to its usual state.

The **Task to Aid Mindfulness** this week is to be completed straight after the meditation. This is because the meditation is aimed to relax you and we are more aware of our true selves when we are relaxed.

Now I want you to think of a habit that you have that you would like to get rid of. This could be anything at all from the usual such as stopping smoking or eating the wrong foods, to secret habits such as picking your nose whilst watching TV alone at home at night.

Think about the habit and think about:

- How often you carry out the habit.

- The circumstances that lead to the habit being carried out.

Now close your eyes and imagine that you are watching yourself in a movie. Think about the last time that you carried out the habit and see it being played in the movie. Now be honest with yourself. Ask yourself what you were thinking, become aware of your thoughts and what you did that led to the habit being carried out.

Now pay attention to your thoughts and then let everything go that you have been holding onto by taking a deep breath in through your nose and out through your mouth.

You may now go about your day and return to the exercise tomorrow and for the rest of the week.

WEEK 4

This week you will concentrate on showing compassion towards yourself and towards other people. This week is about helping you to live well.

Too many of us work too hard and beat ourselves up when we become tired or ill. Often we find that as we near exhaustion we become bad tempered and our close relationships become affected. Mindfulness meditations allow you to see things as they really are. This week we will firstly focus on a meditation which will help you remember who you really are at your core.

Connecting With Your Core Mindfulness Meditation

- Go to the place where you usually carry out your meditation. Remember to place your feet flat on the floor and sit up so that you are not slouching.

- Take a deep breath in through you nose and as you exhale I want you to close your eyes and relax.

- Now keep breathing at a slightly slower and relaxed place.

- As you continue to breathe in this way you find yourself sinking deeper and deeper into a beautiful relaxed state.

- When you are ready I want you to think about an activity or hobby that you had that you wished that you had time for now.

- Think about this activity or hobby and in your mind imagine that you are carrying it out right now.

- Stay focused on this for a few minutes.

- Now, take a deep breath in in through your nose and release the visualisation.

- When you are ready, open your eyes and bring your focus back into the room around you.

- Now ask yourself why you no longer carry out activity or hobby that brings you so much joy.

If your answer is that you no longer have the time then you know that is really an excuse. This week I want you to carry out at least one activity that brings the feeling of joy to your heart. This is an essential exercise DO NOT UNDERESTIMATE ITS IMPORTANCE. Not only does feeling joyful and happy help maintain good health by realising endorphins into the blood, happy people are less likely to become ill than unhappy stressed people.

This week be compassionate towards yourself by giving yourself the gift of time and may be surprised at the results.

Tasks to Aid Mindfulness
Be kind and compassionate to others; when someone is telling you of a difficult situation that they have experienced, even though you may feel the need in your mind to judge that person, show compassion instead. Notice how much better you feel when you show compassion.

Be kind and compassionate to yourself: buy yourself a small gift, allow yourself a lovely relaxing bath or just spending time reading your favourite book.

When you are compassionate to yourself you are really acknowledging that you are an important person and that you value yourself.

Compassion, in my opinion is an important part not only of mindfulness but also an important characteristic of the Reiki practitioner. Is it any wonder that Mikao Usui included being compassionate in the Reiki precepts?

AN EVALUATION

Now that you have carried out the 4 week Mindfulness programme ask yourself if you feel that it has been beneficial to you. Be honest with yourself. If you have found that it has not, is that because you did not carry out the programme as suggested or for some other reason?

The information contained within this book regarding Mindfulness is meant to act as a beginners guide only. If you are interested in studying Mindfulness further there are many books available which will support you in your learning.

HOW TO CARRY OUT A PROFESSIONAL REIKI TREATMENT A STEP BY STEP GUIDE

When individuals have been connected to the Reiki source at first degree level they may carry out treatments on family and friends. If an individual intends to work as a Reiki practitioner they must complete the second degree level after which the individual is able to obtain professional indemnity insurance.

Many students who take Reiki courses are already therapists and it is not uncommon for massage therapists, osteopaths and beauty therapists to study Reiki and offer Reiki treatments as part of their practice after studying the second degree level.

There are, of course, many people from many different professional and non-professional backgrounds who study Reiki and this first part of the guide is really written with them in mind.

When my students study Reiki first degree I encourage them to get as much practice on family and friends as possible. This is really for 2 reasons:

1. To notice how one person's energy feels different to another person's.

2. To make your Reiki stronger – remember practice increases strength!

The Working Environment
Before you begin your practice you will need to find a suitable place to carry out your treatments. This could be a spare room in your home, or perhaps even your living room temporarily converted into a therapy room. It does not matter where you practice but it does matter that the room is quiet and that you will not have any distractions whilst you are carrying out the treatment. To this end ensure that all telephones and electrical equipment is turned off.

If you do not already have one it is very wise to invest in a therapy couch; many people try to carry out treatments on a bed or sofa and end up hurting their back in the process. A portable lightweight therapy couch is ideal if you intend to move the couch around from one place to the next quite a lot. These couches are very affordable and you can easily purchase one online. If you do this it may be wise to check out any reviews of the product, or the seller, before you purchase. I know of at least one therapist who purchased a couch which was described as lightweight and when the couch was delivered to her found that it was anything but. Also be aware of any second hand or previously owned couches. These may appear to be a lot cheaper but they may arrive damaged and stained.

Finally check maximum weight that the couch can hold. You certainly do not want the couch to collapse if it is unable to hold a person because they are too heavy for it. Not only is it embarrassing for the client they may hurt themselves and hold you liable.

Naturally you will want to make the room and the atmosphere as inviting, relaxing and attractive as possible. Some therapists choose to use relaxing music. There is a wide choice available including music specifically for Reiki practitioners. Choose something that you can fully merge with and which you feel helps your Reiki become stronger. Ensure that the music is not too loud and that the client does not have an objection to it.

Candles and incense: again, these are used to help relaxation and to add to the experience of the Reiki treatment. Check that your client does not have asthma or other allergies.

A little note: although you are only working on family and friends at the moment it is still possible that you may not be aware that an individual has allergies or similar. It is important to check as you do not want to cause discomfort to anyone during any of your treatments.

Check List

- Working space – is it quiet? Review room for potential disturbances.

- Check weight of couch, maximum weight it can hold, check reviews if purchasing online.

- Are you using music? If so is it suitable? Does the client have any objections?

- Candles/incense – safety – check that the client does not have any allergies/objections.

The Therapist
Most of this applies to ladies but if you are a gentleman please have a read through as some of this is applicable to you.

Please ensure when you are treating others that you:

- Wear appropriate clothing: No fancy sleeves on dresses or blouses which could irritate a client by flapping or falling over the clients face or body causing irritation.

- Do not wear low cut tops – this looks unprofessional as well as possibly causing a distraction.

- Do not wear strong perfume which could irritate a client.

- Remember to be fresh - an application of deodorant may be especially appreciated during the warmer weather.

- Foot wear: Do not wear high heels. You will not be able to carry out an effective treatment and your back will be killing you! Wear socks if at all possible. You will be well grounded and an excess energy will return to the earth.

- Always treat your client regardless of whether the client is a family member friend or anyone else with the utmost of respect. This is a good way for you to practice working with Reiki in a professional manner. It will also show others that you are serious about working with Reiki.

Record Keeping
When working as a professional Reiki practitioner it is essential that you keep records of your clients. This is of course, essential after you have completed the second degree and in general it is requirement placed on you by your insurance company.

At first degree level it a wise idea to begin your record keeping now. You could devise your own record sheets. Here is a simple example to help you get started.

Please remember that we as Reiki practitioners are not qualified to offer medical advice. If a person comments that they are in some way concerned about their health it is wise to suggest that they seek professional medical advice.

Consultation Card

Name: ……………………………………

Contact Numbers:

Mobile: ……………………………………

Home: ……………………………………

Address: ……………………………………

                ……………………………………

                ……………………………………

Health Problems

……………………………………………………………

……………………………………………………………

……………………………………………………………

Reiki Sessions (comments)

Session 1

....

....

....

Session 2

....

....

....

Session 3

....

....

....

The Treatment

A full body treatment takes around 50 to 60 minutes. Stay in each position for 3 to 5 minutes to begin with. You may spend less time in each position if you intend to work on the back as well. Please read through the whole of this section at least once before beginning your treatment.

Please note: Ask your client to remove their shoes and any chunky jewellery before lying on the couch. You may need to help your client onto the couch if they are elderly, have a physical injury or are disabled in any way. You may also find that you need to raise the top of the couch to support the clients head. This may be due to a respiratory condition such as asthma, or simply because the client feels uncomfortable even with the head rest supporting them. Please remember to ask the client if they are comfortable before you begin the treatment. Unless you ask, many will not tell you even if they are not! I tend to use a blanket when carrying out my treatments. I believe that this helps the client relax more fully as the blanket helps them to feel secure. The use of a blanket does not "block" the Reiki energy in any way.

Some Reiki practitioners work better "hands on" the client and others "hands off" the client. I myself work much better "hands off". It really does not matter which way you work. There are teachers and other practitioners who will state that you must always work "hands on" or always work "hands off" and this is really not the case. What is important is the preference of the client. Most clients simply want a good treatment but others will state a preference, especially if they do prefer not to be touched at all and you must respect that. Some people do not want their feet touched as it drives them a little crazy!

Even if you work "hands off" the client most of the time you may feel the need to make physical contact, say, when working on the hips for example. As a beginner this may be a little hard to understand at the moment but with practice you will begin to realise what I mean as your intuition develops. The best way to address this is before the client's first treatment. Say something like this at the start of the treatment:

"I mostly work hands off during the treatment session but sometimes I do place my hands on the body, for example on the thighs. Is that okay with you? I won't be placing my hands on any intimate areas. I am just saying this to put your mind at rest".

Finally, a client may not be sure if they should keep awake or close their eyes. Just before you begin say something like:

"You may want to close your eyes now or in a few minutes time when you begin to relax. Don't worry if you fall asleep. At the end of the session I will gently wake you up by touching your arm and telling you that the treatment has ended."

In this way the client knows what is expected of him/her and they can now relax and enjoy the session.

Important: YOU must feel relaxed before you begin a Reiki treatment. It is important to remember that you cannot rush around and then hurry to begin the treatment. You will not be able to give the best treatment possible if your mind is elsewhere. Some Reiki practitioners begin by taking a few deep breaths and focusing themselves first. Others imagine that Reiki is cascading all of the way from the crown down to the hands and out towards the client. Some practitioners simply rub their hands together to stimulate the energy before they begin.

VERY, VERY IMPORTANT!

When you work with the energy your mind must be as relaxed as possible, this is why it is important that you carry out the meditations on a regular basis. It is also important that you do not have any expectations. The Reiki energy will do what is needed for the client at that particular time. The energy will work for the good of the client in as far as the client will allow it to work. You, as a Reiki practitioner are simply a vessel for which the Reiki to flow through.

Begin by Scanning

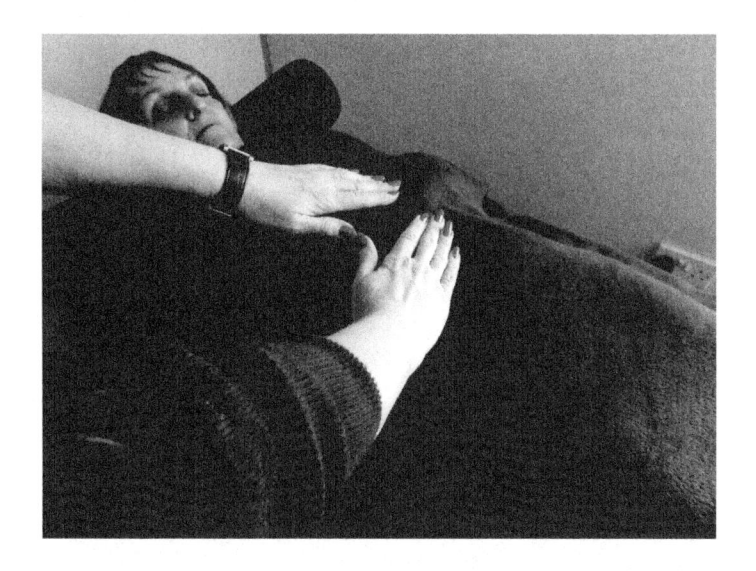

Scanning allows you to get a feel for the client's energy field. Begin at the top of the head on the left or right side of the body (it really does not matter which side).

Place your hands a few inches from the body and slowly sweep down the body all the way to the toes.

Repeat from the head to the torso in the middle of the body.

And finally the other side.

When you are scanning remember to move your hands at a slow even pace. When you are scanning you may feel some areas of hot or cold or perhaps you will feel tingling sensations in your hands or finger tips. This will vary from client to client and from treatment to treatment. Tingling, hot, cold or buzzing sensations indicate where there is an energy imbalance.

Connect With the Client

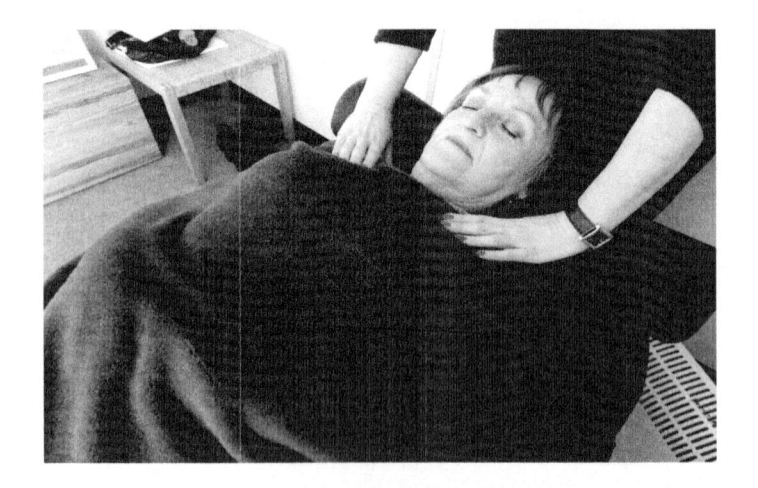

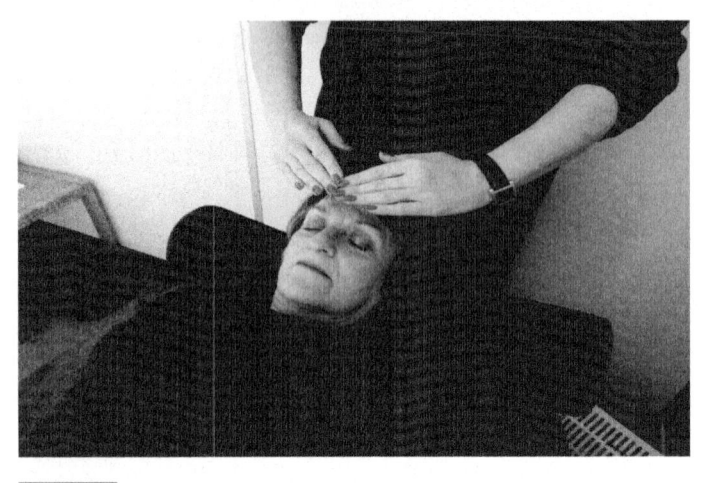

This is where you will begin to connect with the client's energy and where you will begin to build up the flow of Reiki. Your hands can be placed on the client's shoulders or with your hands in a sort of bridge position over the forehead. I tend to use the latter because I feel that I get a better connection in this way. In addition, some clients may feel that, with your hands on their shoulder, they feel held or forced down. When you are working professionally you will not know the background of most of your clients. With your hands on the shoulder position some clients may be remind of unpleasant past experiences.

Hands Over The Face

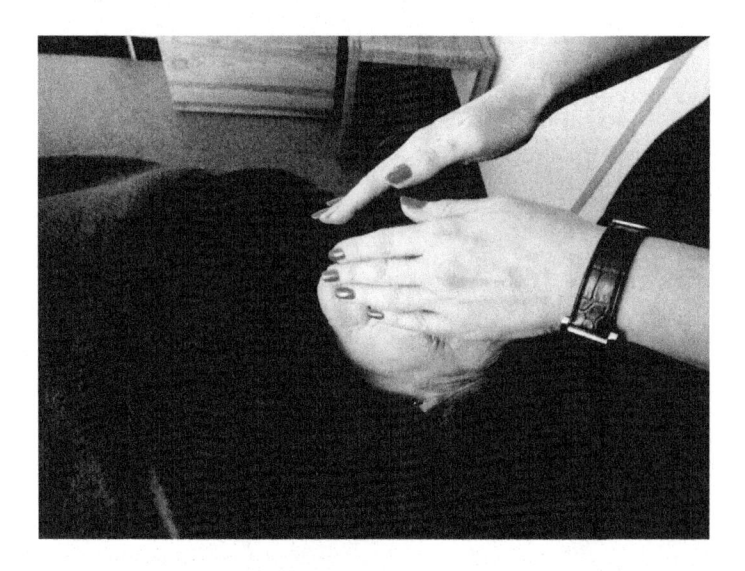

This is one of my favourite hand positions. It reminds me of a ray of sunshine and it allows the client to relax any tension in the face.

Hands at the Sides of the Temples

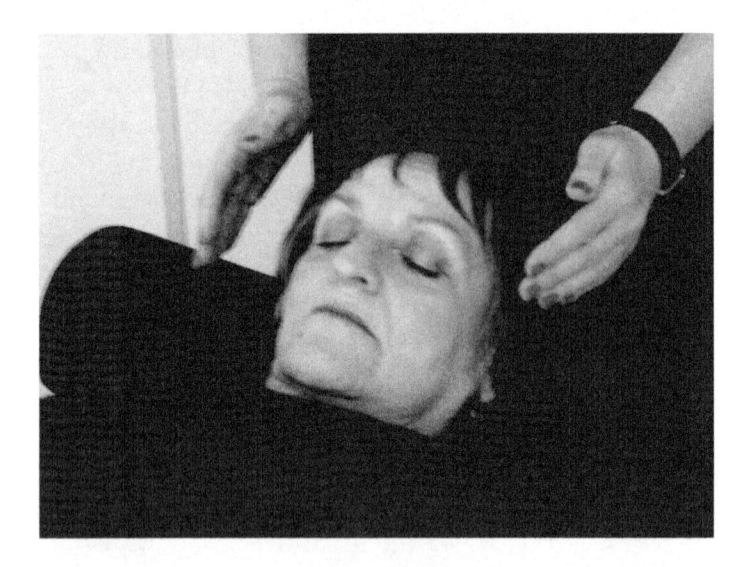

Place the hands a couple of inches from the temples. As your intuition develops your hands will automatically "know" where to be positioned.

Hands Over the Crown

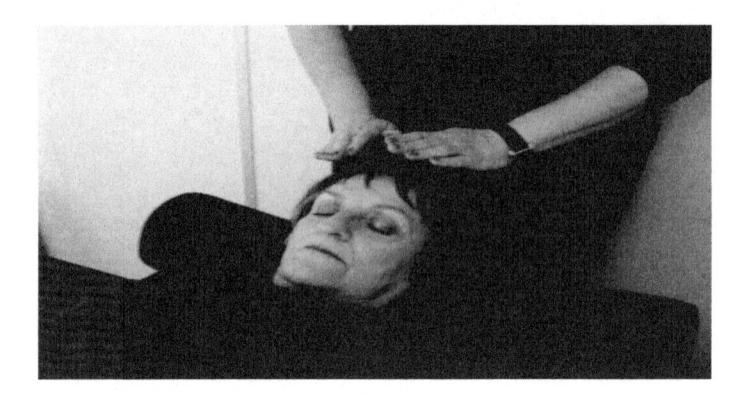

Again, place then hands a couple of inches over the crown. Often I find that if the person is a worrier there is a lot of heat generated in this area.

Forehead & Back of the Head

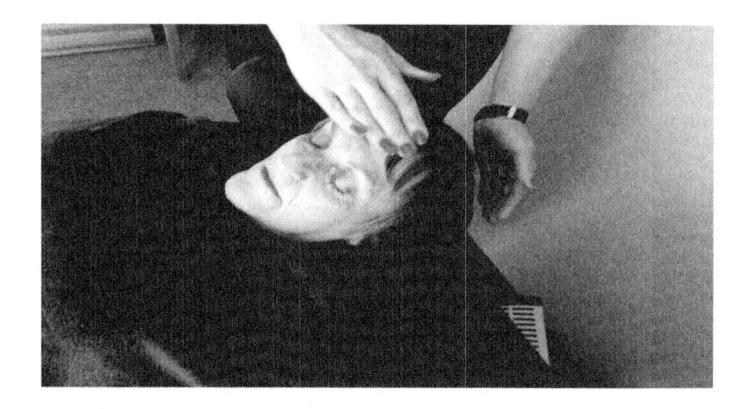

Place on hand a couple of inches over the crown and the other hand a couple of inches below the back of the head.

Throat

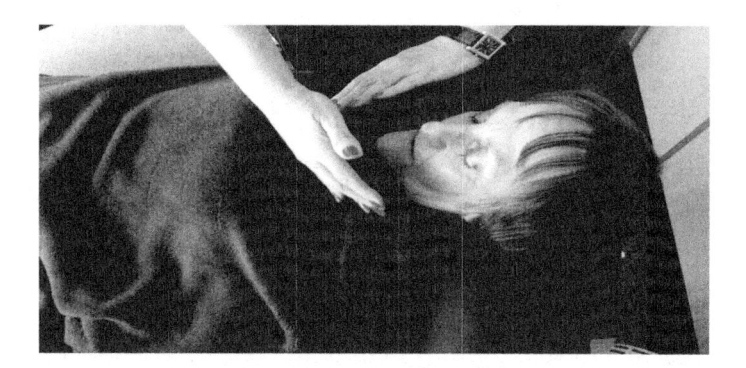

Place one hand a couple of inches away from each side of the throat. Caution: Some clients begin to swallow, cough or even choke during this hand position. If the discomfort appears to be slight, then simply move your hands further away or separate your fingers in order to release some of the energy. If the client is in obvious discomfort then move on to the next hand position.

The Heart & Solar Plexus

From this hand position onwards you may work hands on or hands off the client. See the note at the beginning of this section as a reminder if necessary. Place your hands on or over the heart area. When you are ready, move on to the solar plexus.

The Hips

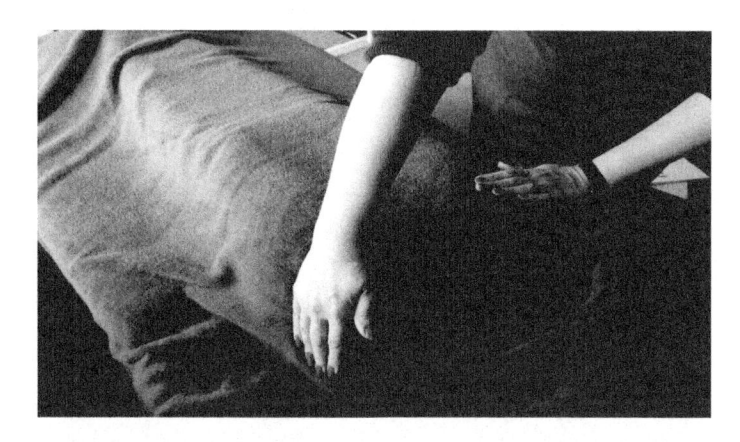

Place the hands on or over each side of the hips.

The Thighs

Place your hands on or over each of the thighs.

The Feet

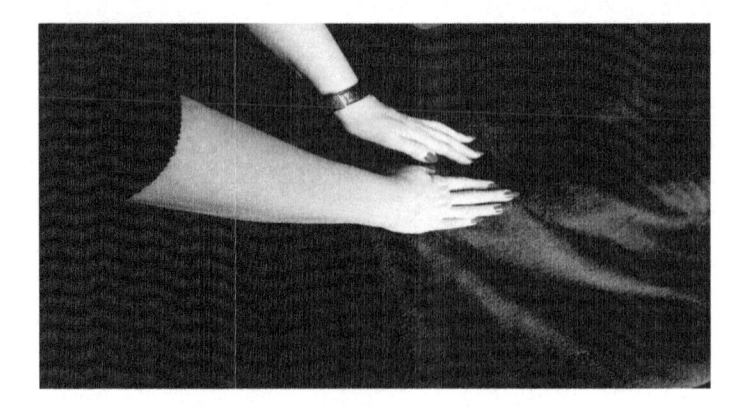

Place your hands over or on each of the feet. Note: Some people have very sensitive feet. It is wise to ask the client if it okay to touch the feet if it is our intention to do so.

Back Positions
Some Reiki teachers state that it is essential to carry out treatment on the back as it is part of a complete treatment. Others state that this is not so and that by asking the client to turn around is both disruptive to both the therapist and to the client. The client may have to be woken up and asked to turn over and the therapist has a disruption to the flow of the energy. I myself hardly ever treat the back unless the client has a specific back problem.

A couch is essential for carrying out the back positions. The client needs to keep the neck straight and not twisted to the side which could cause discomfort or injury. Most couches have a gap through which the client can place their head during back treatments, in this way the spine is kept straight.

Here are the hand positions for the back for you to follow if you choose to do so. These are all shown with "hands on" the back but you can work "hands off" as well.

A note of caution: never, ever apply any pressure to the back as this may result in injury. Never work direction on the spine itself as again, this may result in injury.

The Neck

Hands on or over each side of the neck.

The Shoulder Blades and Lower Back

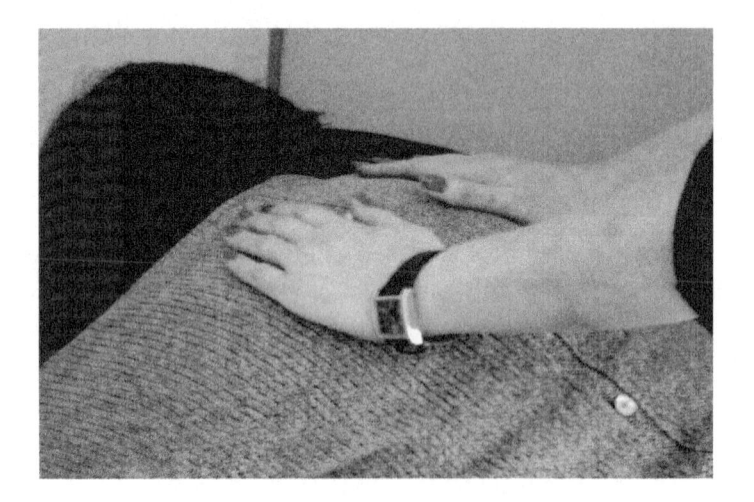

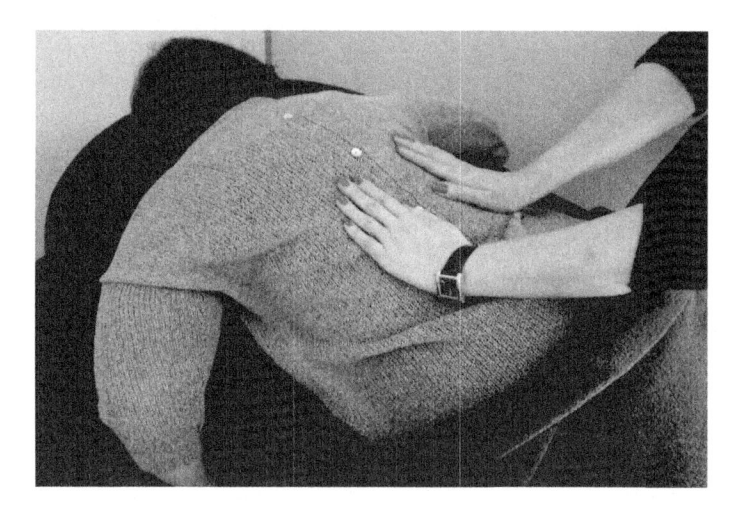

Gently work at each side of the spine.

Base of the Spine

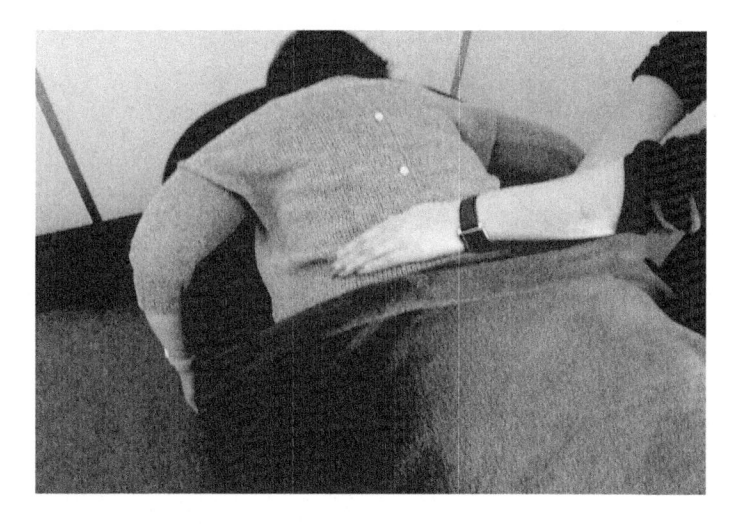

Finish by placing one hand at each side of the base of the spine.

You may finish the treatment by gently touching the clients arm and informing him or her that the treatment has ended.

A note about hand positions
The hand positions in this book are those that I have found to be the most beneficial both to myself as the therapist and to the client. There are other hand positions shown in other books. Although it is important to be able to work on others by carrying out Reiki treatments it is equally important not to be too concerned about hand positions. As you progress, if that is your intention, you will be less concerned with the standard hand positions because your intuition will guide you as to where you want to work. The hand positions are really to get you started. In some ways they act as a comfort blanket for you. Your mind does not get in the way of the Reiki treatment by worrying about which hand position you need to carry out next.

REIKI & YOU

Including:

- Daily Energy Exercises

    &

- Reiki Self Treatments

WORK ON YOURSELF: DAILY ENERGY EXERCISES

There are 2 energy exercises that Usui taught his students. There are called:

Kenyoku – this mean dry bathing or brushing off.

Joshin Kokkyu Ho - This is a technique for purification of the spirit or the soul; a cleansing and bathing method.

These exercises can be combined (along with a few others) so that the student can carry out Hatsurei Ho. This exercise takes 10 – 15 minutes to complete. This exercise was originally revealed to the west by Hiroshi Doi in 1999.

The following pages show the complete movements for Hatsurei Ho. I have written out the series of movements for Kenyoku and Joshin Kokkyu Ho. These can be carried out as separate exercises. Some of my students do these exercises instead of carrying out the Hatsurei Ho exercise if they do not have the time to carry out the complete routine.

Hatsurei Ho

As usual, find a comfortable and quiet place where you can carry out this exercise. Ensure that you will not be disturbed and remember to turn off your mobile phone.

Place your hands, palms down in your lap.

Close your eyes and take a deep breath in through the nose and out through the mouth.

Feel that you are "centring" yourself.

When you do this you are focusing on the lower Tanden. This is called the Dantian in Chinese. This is your energy centre, your life force and is located a few centimetres below you belly button. There are also 2 other Tanden locations. These are to be found in the middle of the chest and between the eyebrows.

Acknowledge to yourself that you are now carrying out the Hatsurei Ho exercise. Say to yourself either silently or out loud:

"I am beginning the Hatsurei Ho exercise now"

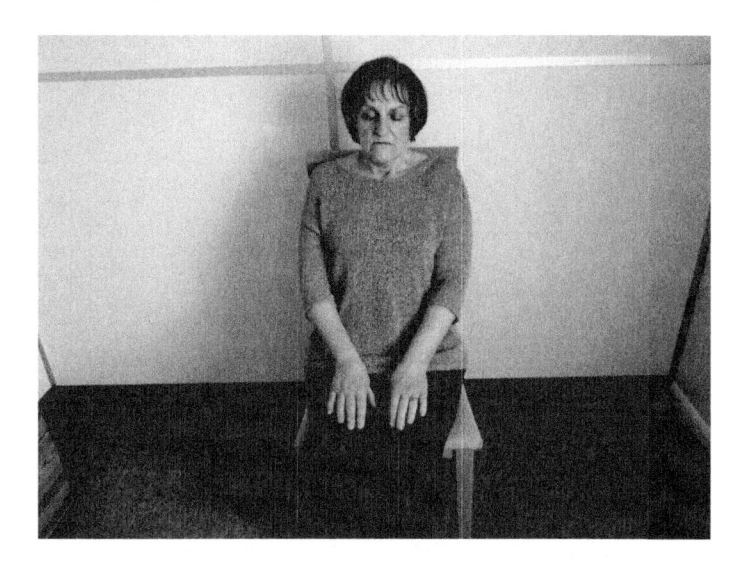

Now begin the dry bathing:

Start with your right hand on the left shoulder.

Keep your fingertips together.

Sweep across the chest to the hip.

Place your hand on your knee palms down.

Now repeat with the left hand on the right shoulder.

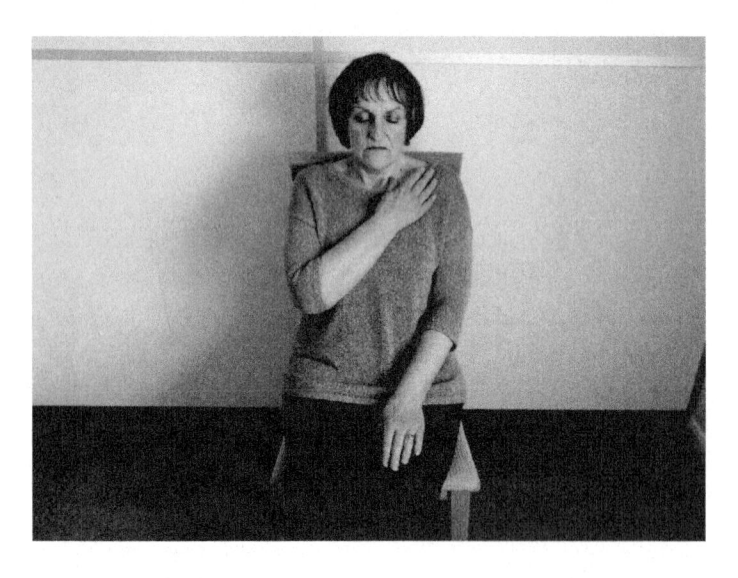

Repeat this: left hand on right shoulder, sweep to the hip and repeat with the right hand on the left shoulder once move. This makes a total of 3 sweeps.

Now place your right hand on the left shoulder again.

Stretch your left arm out straight.

Now sweep all the way down the left arm, almost like you are brushing something away.

Repeat on the other side.

Now repeat by placing the right hand on the left shoulder once more. This makes a total of 3 sweeps.

As you carry out the exercise imagine that you are clearing away negative energy and negative thoughts.

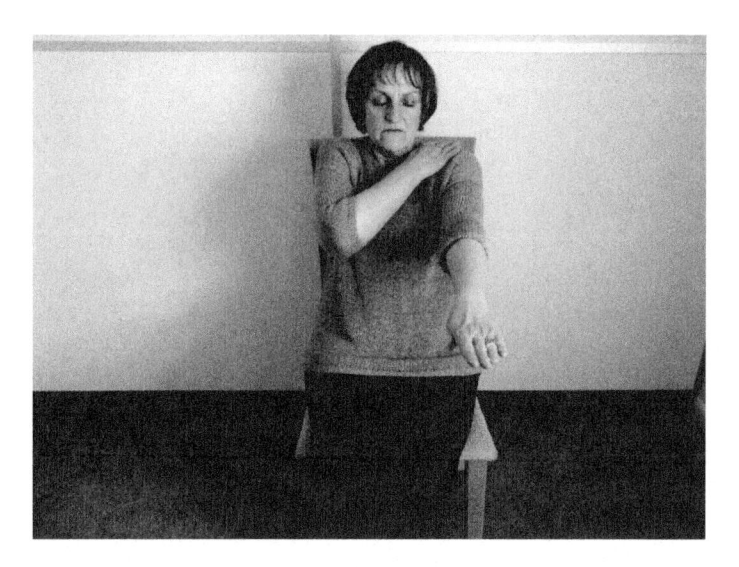

Now raise your hands above your head.

You are connecting to the source of energy. Feel and imagine the light shining down on you.

If you have a disability and have problems raising your hands to this level do not worry. You can simply raise your hands as far as is comfortable. It is your thoughts and intentions that are important when you carry out this exercise.

Stay with your hands in this position for a minute or so if you can, or until you feel a strong connection to Reiki.

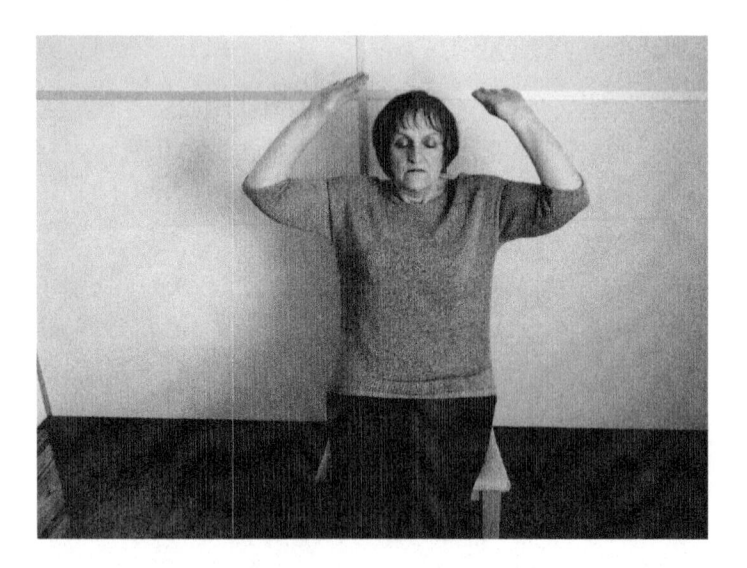

Now pop your hands back into your lap.

As you breathe in imagine that you are breathing in pure healing energy, pure light which goes all the way down your body from the crown of your head to your lower Tanden.

As you breathe out you are breathing out all of the stress, tension and worry that you have been holding onto.

Keep breathing in this way for a few minutes.

Notice how relaxed you feel.

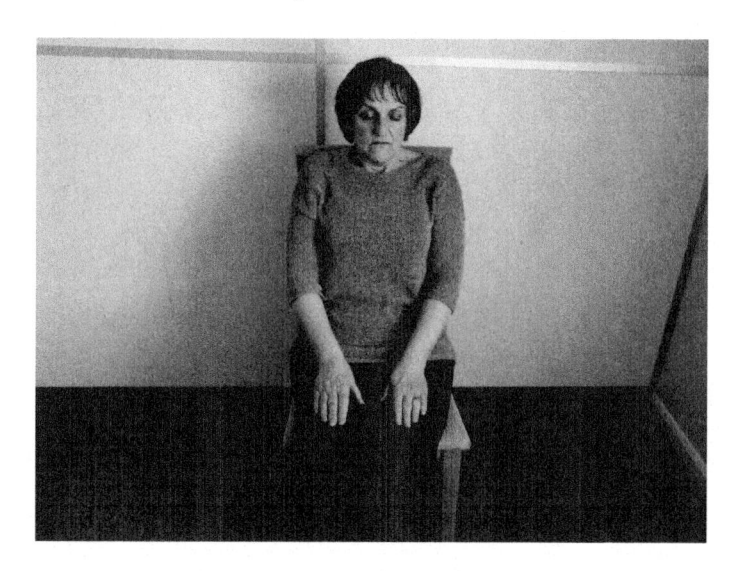

Now put your hands in the prayer position.

If you have physical difficulty holding this position for several minutes you may wish to use support cushions under your arms or perhaps rolled up towels.

Become aware of your fingers.

Pay particular attention to where the middle fingers meet. Focus on the pads of those fingers.

Now focus on your breathing.

As you breathe in imagine energy going all the way down from the crown of the head to the hands.

From the hands, the energy flows to the lower Tanden.

Now breathe out.

Feel the energy flowing from the lower Tanden up to the hands and out to the universe.

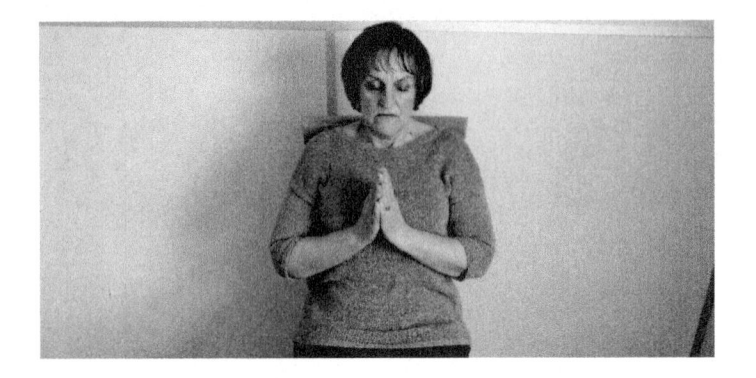

Now place your hands, palms down onto your lap.

Stay in this position and centre yourself once again.

When you are ready say either out loud or to yourself:

"The Hatsurei Ho exercise has ended now"

When you are ready take a long deep breath.

Open your eyes and stay in this position for a few minutes until you become fully alert and awake.

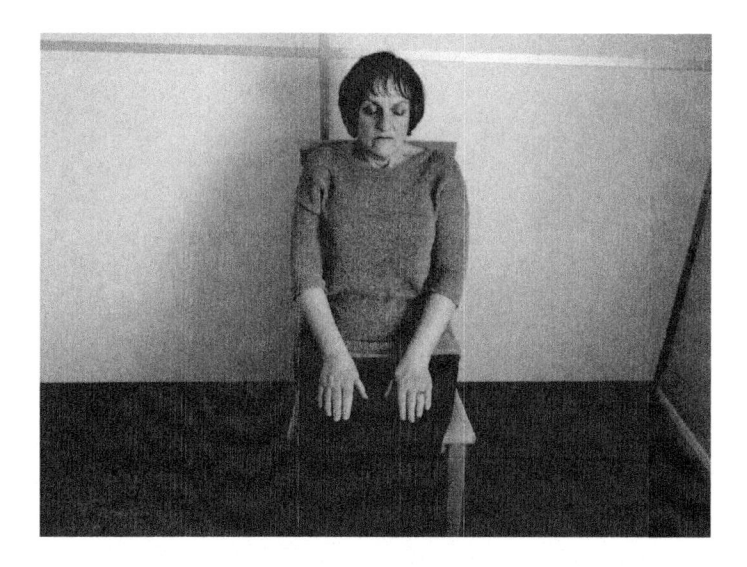

REIKI SELF TREATMENTS

A great way to practice and strengthen your Reiki is to carry out a Reiki self-treatment. The purpose of this is to:

- Strengthen your connection to the Reiki source.

- Make your Reiki stronger.

- Aid your concentration as you really focus on the point or position that you are sending Reiki to.

Usui encouraged his students to carry out daily self-healing exercises and it may be assumed that he did so for all of the reasons listed above.

Reiki self-treatments may be carried out by placing your hands on various points or positions on your body. You can also carry out self-healing by visualisation: simply imagine that energy is being sent to various parts of the body.

Below I have described the most common head positions. Remember that self-healing can be carried out anywhere on your body. All you have to do is to focus and send the energy to where you want it to go. Try it and see for yourself. Try to maintain each position for between 3 and 5 minutes. If you have any difficulty, either because you physically cannot hold your arms in these positions or for some other reason, try the visualisation exercises instead as the results are the same.

Begin by playing your hands in the Gassho position and focusing your attention.

Begin to feel the Reiki cascading down to your hands from the crown of your head.

When you feel the energy flowing to the fingertips remind yourself that this is your time to self-heal.

Feel the glow of warmth as you bathe your face in Reiki energy. Feel the muscles relax.

Place the hands at the top of the head. Feel the warmth and energy generate down in to the skull.

Place the hands at the sides of the head. Feel any tension in the temples slowly melt away. This position is great to help reduce/eliminate headaches.

Above are the two Reiki hand positions for the throat. You may decide to use one or both. Feel the energy in the throat and feel the muscles relax.

There are other hand positions on the head; one of these is placing the hands at the back of the skull. I and many of my students find that position quite difficult and that is the reason that I have not pictured it in this book. If you are uncomfortable the Reiki will not work well. It is far better that you visualise Reiki going to the back of the skull if that is where you intend to send it rather than have aching arms while trying to hold that position.

OTHERS WAYS TO WORK WITH REIKI

Reiki Your Food
This is a great way to make your food taste better. Simply serve your food on a plate and place your hands over the plate for a few minutes. It really does work, try it and see. If you want a little challenge try sending Reiki to the food on some days and not others, you will notice the difference. If you live in a household with other people, set them a test by telling them that you are going to send Reiki to their food on some days and not others. At the end of the day ask them to guess if you had sent Reiki that day or not.

Reiki Your Plants
If you have plants in your home you can help them look better and live longer by sending them Reiki. If you are growing a plant from seeds you can Reiki the seeds before planting by placing the seeds in your hand and sending them Reiki. As the plant begins to grow, you can Reiki the soil to help the plant to grow. As the plant grows, feel around its energy field by tracing the outline of the leaves or flowers of the plant with your hands. You may notice that some plants start to shake a little. You may feel areas of imbalance, areas of increased heat and cold patches in the same way that you may feel these changes in energy in a human or an animal. This is because the plant has an energy field as well.

Try sending Reiki to the plant now. The amount of time you spend doing this is up to you but I would suggest 5 minutes minimum. Some people find this a very relaxing and therapeutic way to send Reiki and I am sure that the plant will appreciate it as well.

Send Reiki to Your Animals
I simply adore animals and at the time of writing I have 3 dogs and 2 cats. You really cannot predict how an animal will react to Reiki. For example, Jessie, one of my border collies, will tolerate it for a few minutes and then walk away. Bones, my border terrier, will sit with you all day long if he can have Reiki or if I am giving a treatment at home. Alfie, my other border collie, does not like it and leaves the room as soon as he senses the energy.

If you are working with an animal for the first time here are a few tips to help you get started:

Do not corner or box the animal in no matter how well you know it. If you do this you will cause the animal a great deal of stress. Ensure that it has a way to escape if it feels uncomfortable or overwhelmed by the energy.

If the animal is a dog it may be wise, if possible, to take the dog for a walk before giving it Reiki .This is to ensure that any excess energy is burnt off and therefore the dog is more likely to relax when receiving the treatment.

If you are working with your animal, sit next to it perhaps on the floor or the sofa. Imagine Reiki energy cascading from the crown all the way to your hands. Now feel the Reiki radiating from your hands.

Scan the body of the animal in the same way you would if you were treating a human client.

Hold your hands over any areas which you feel you would like to treat or any areas where you detect an energy imbalance.

Please note that this may seem easier than it actually is; I am writing from experience here! Jessie for example does not like Reiki over her back leg and she will pull my hand away. I believe that she needs Reiki in this area so it is only with determination and patience that I keep going back and working on this area as she has a little arthritis in her legs. I have known other dogs feel so relaxed that they will turn over on their backs and wriggle whilst others will lick your hands as a way of saying thank you. Whilst this may be their way of showing you that they adore the Reiki it can really disrupt your treatment. Try to treat for 5 minutes in each area or hand position that you work on if possible.

When working on an animal that you do not know, especially if the animal is nervous, remember to sit some distance away from it. You can begin by imagining and feeling Reiki cascading from the crown, down the body and out of the hands. You can feel the energy filling the room and radiating outwards towards the animal. This will help to relax and calm the animal and often it will come little closer to you. I have even known animals to come and sit next to the person generating the Reiki. This almost seems that animal is asking for a Reiki treatment. How lovely!

Please remember that you must respect the animal that you are treating, regardless of whether it is a dog or a hamster. You cannot force Reiki on any living thing and the animal will only accept the Reiki if it wants it at that time. If you are unsuccessful the first time try again another day. Please also remember that Reiki is not intended as a medical substitute and any animal that is sick or suspected of being ill or who is injured or in pain should be taken to a veterinarian straight away. Reiki does work well with animals who are stressed, anxious and who have had surgery as it may aid/support healing. Please also be aware of your own personal safety. If an animal is afraid or aggressive it may attack.

If you are interested in working with the Reiki energy with animals there are many courses specifically for this. A quick search online will naturally point you in the right directions. When you have found a course that is appealing please remember to carry out a quick search for reviews. These courses are sometimes quite expensive and I am sure that you would want to spend your money wisely.

Reiki the bus, train, the room and any other public place!

When you are out and about try this exercise. Centre yourself and if you can, close your eyes for a couple of minutes. Begin by feeling the energy cascading all the way down from the crown and out of your hands. Then feel the energy drifting from the hands, like small clouds, out in to the atmosphere all around you.

I have done this exercise many times and often you actually see people begin to relax all around you. I have also tried this at meetings with the same results. This is a wonderful way to help people to relax. Remember that as the energy enters a person's energy field they will only accept the Reiki if they want to. The energy will not do any harm and will work for the benefit of the person who receives it.

Remember to be creative with Reiki; you may be surprised with the results. The only limitations that are placed on the use of it are those that we place on ourselves.

THE FIVE KEYS TO REIKI

There are five aspects or keys to Reiki which should be followed by anyone who is:

- Serious about working with the energy.

- Wishing to progress spiritually.

- Intending to move on the second degree and beyond.

I call the following steps the five keys because a key opens a door and each step or key will open your own door for you. Each key is an on-going process. Life is not static. No matter how much you may wish to keep things the same when life is good or change things when life is not so good. As you take a step through each of the five doors your life will begin to change. For some it will occur more quickly than others. Change is often subtle at first. Try it and see for yourself.

The Precepts

Place your hands in the Gassho position both morning and evening. Say the Reiki precepts. I have written them out below for you as a reminder:

For Today Only:

Do not anger.

Do not worry.

Be humble

Be honest with other people and in your work

Be compassionate to yourself and others.

As you say these words either to yourself or out loud you are making a commitment that you will be in control of your behaviour and your responses. You are building subtle energy in your lower Tanden.

Meditation
Please remember to carry out your daily meditations. I have already discussed at some length the importance of meditation and how to carry out your meditations correctly. Even just a few minutes a day will be beneficial.

Hands On Healing
Try working on others whenever the opportunity arises, you will learn so much about other people and their energy. You will also receive the Reiki so you will have a treatment too. Working on other people is your way of giving back to the community, society and the universe.

Healing Self-Treatments
Work on yourself at least once a week, more if time allows. Giving yourself Reiki is a way of truly connecting with yourself on a deeply emotional level. You will begin to appreciate your whole body and the parts of it that make it whole: your heart, your lungs and your liver and so on. All parts of you that enable you to function and keep your physical body alive.

Reiju Empowerments
I send all of my students Reiju empowerments on a Sunday. If you are reading this book as part of a distant learning course then this also applies to you. If you have studied Reiki elsewhere then please contact your teacher and enquire about Reiju empowerments.

Reiki shares are also a great idea of connecting with Reiki people in your area. They are ideal for bringing like-minded people together. If there is not one in your area you may consider setting one up yourself.

SECOND DEGREE?

Many students often ask me the question: "When will I be ready for the second degree?"

My advice is always the same: please work with the energy and on other people as much as you can. You need to wait for a period of between three and six months, this is because:

- The energy needs time to settle down after you have received your empowerments as it has affected you to a greater or lesser degree physically and emotionally.

- You need time to practice energy work both on yourself and on others. You need to carry out the five keys on a regular basis.

I never teach the first and second degree levels together for these reasons. I try to keep as close to the traditional methods as possible by allowing my students the time they need before helping them on their journey via the second degree.

I advise a period of three to six months because each person is an individual. For some they become comfortable and confident working with the energy and are ready in three months. For others it is longer. As a person becomes more self-aware and intuitive they know in their hearts when they are ready to move forward on their Reiki journey.

ABOUT THE AUTHOR

Marion McGeough is a Reiki Master currently living in Derbyshire, England. She is also a psychotherapist with practices in Ashby De La Zouch, Leicestershire and Sutton Coldfield, West Midlands.

Marion is also the author of:

A Beginner's Guide to the Chakras

Crystal healing and the Human Energy Field: A Beginner's Guide

Hypnosis CD:

Overcome Your Fear of Flying

All products can be purchased on Amazon

For further information about Reiki, or about the range of Reiki courses or treatments she offers, Marion can be contacted via her website: www.britishacademyofreiki.co.uk

Printed in Great Britain
by Amazon